THE WILLIAM CAMPBELL DOUGLASS LETTERS

William Campbell Douglass II, MD

Rhino Publishing, S.A.

THE WILLIAM CAMPBELL DOUGLASS LETTERS

Copyright © 1968, 2003
by
William Campbell Douglass II, MD

ISBN 9962-636-46-9

Cover illustration by
Alex Manyoma (alex@3dcity.com)

Please, visit Rhino's website for other publications from
Dr. William Campbell Douglass
www.rhinopublish.com

Dr. Douglass' "Real Health" alternative medical
newsletter is available at www.realhealthnews.com

RHINO PUBLISHING, S.A.
World Trade Center
Panama, Republic of Panama
Voicemail/Fax
International: + 416-352-5126
North America: 888-317-6767

It is not what a lawyer tells me I may do;
but what humanity, reason, and justice,
tell me I ought to do.

Edmund Burke, March 1775

PREFACE

What happens to me is not important. But it is important that some Americans stand up in the spirit of John Hampdon of England and Patrick Henry of America and refuse to wear the yoke of a tax slave. It has been said that the highest price a man can pay in defending his country is to give his life. But there is a higher price. He can give up his precious freedom and go to jail. He can go to the living hell of an iron cage rather than submit to an evil system of taxation that is sucking the life's blood from his children.

I do not anticipate going to jail, however, because I have committed no crime and debtors' prisons are illegal in our country. What will happen next I do not know--it is the bureaucracy's move.

William Campbell Douglass, MD
Sarasota, Florida
April 15, 1968

"Strange that cowards cannot see that their greatest safety lies in dauntless courage. " -- Xenophon

Form 1040

U.S. Individual Income Tax Return 1965

For the year January 1–December 31, 1965 or other taxable year beginning _____ 1965, ending _____, 19 ____ US Treasury Department—Internal Revenue Service

If joint return, use first names and middle initials of both)

Last name

William C. DOUGLASS

Home address and street or (rural route)

1712 Hillview

(City, town or post office, and State)

Postal ZIP code

Sarasota Fla.

Enter name and address used on your return for 1964 (if the same as above, write "Same"). If none filed, give reason. If changing from separate to joint or joint to separate return, enter 1964 names and addresses.

Your social security number (Husband's if joint return)

Your occupation & present employer

Wife's number, if joint return

Wife's occupation & present employer

Filing Status—check one:

- 1a ☐ Single
- 1b ☐ Married filing joint return (even if only one had income)
- 1c ☐ Married filing separately. If your husband or wife is also filing a return give his or her first name and social security number.
- 1d ☐ Unmarried Head of Household
- 1e ☐ Surviving widow(er) with dependent child

Exemptions

	Regular	Blind	65 or over
2a Yourself	☐	☐	☐
2b Wife	☐	☐	☐

Enter number of exemptions checked ▶ ▲

3a First names of your dependent children who lived with you.

Enter number ▶ ▲

3b Number of other dependents (from page 2 Part I, line 3) ▲

4 Total exemptions claimed ▲

- 5 Wages, salaries, tips, etc. If not shown on attached Forms W-2 attach explanation ▲
- 6 Other income (from page 2, Part II, line 9) ▲
- 7 Total (add lines 5 and 6) ▲
- 8 Adjustments (from page 2, Part II, line 5) ▲
- 9 Total income (subtract line 8 from line 7) ▲
- 10 Figure tax by using either line 10 or 11

Tax Table—If you do not itemize deductions and line 9 is less than $5,000, find your tax from tables in instructions. Do not use lines 11 a, b, c, or d. Enter tax on line 12.

► Attach Copy B of Form W-2

vi

11 **Tax Rate Schedule**

11a If you itemize deductions, enter total from page 2, Part IV
If you do not itemize deductions, and line 9 is $5,000 or more enter the larger of:
(1) 10 percent of line 9 or:
(2) $200 ($100 if married and filing separate return) plus $100 for each exemption claimed on line 4, above.
The deduction computed under (1) or (2) is limited to $1,000 ($500 if married and filing separate return.)

11b Subtract line 11a from line 9

11c Multiply total number of exemptions on line 4, above, by $600

11d Subtract line 11c from line 11b. Enter balance on this line. (Figure your tax on this amount by using tax rate schedule on page 11 of instructions.) **Enter tax on line 12.**

Tax 12 Tax (from either Tax Table, see line 10, or Tax Rate Schedule, see line 11)

Credits 13 Total credits (from page 2, Part V, line 5)

Payments 14 Income tax (subtract line 13 from line 12)

15 Self-employment tax (Schedule C-3 or F-1)

16 Total tax (add lines 14 and 15)

17a Total Federal income tax withheld (attach Forms W-2)

17b 1965 Estimated tax payments
(Include 1964 overpayment allowed as a credit) (Office where paid)

17c Total (add lines 17a and 17b)

Tax Due 18 If payments (line 17c) are less than tax (line 16), enter Balance Due. Pay in full with this return.
or Refund 19 If payments (line 17c) are larger than tax (line 16) enter Overpayment

20 Amount of line 19 you wish credited to 1966 Estimated Tax

21 Subtract line 20 from 19. Apply to: ☐ U.S. Savings Bonds, with excess refunded or ☐ Refund only

If either you or your wife worked for more than one employer see page 5 of instructions

Under penalties of perjury, I declare that I have examined this return, including accompanying schedules and statements, and to the best of my knowledge and belief it is true, correct and complete. If prepared by a person other than taxpayer, his declaration is based on all information of which he has any knowledge.

Sign here ► _____ Date _____
If joint return, BOTH HUSBAND AND WIFE MUST SIGN even if only one had income.

Sign here
Signature of preparer other than taxpayer.

_____ Date _____
Address

► Attach Check or Money Order here ◄

vii

FOREWORD

In refusing to pay the income tax, Dr. Douglass has done what thousands of informed, patriotic Americans would do--if they had the courage.

"What is the difference?" critics may ask, "between the position of Dr. Douglass and of Hosea Williams, Ralph Abernathy, Stokeley Carmichael, Rap Brown and other anarchists and insurrectionists who refuse to obey "Bad Laws?" Plenty of difference! In the first place, Dr. Douglass is trying to uphold our highest law: The Constitution of the United States. The little Red Rioting Hoods are also trying to uphold the Constitution--the Constitution of the U.S.S.R. Our Reds and their "Liberal" friends and sponsors are dedicated to undermining our Constitution and our Republic, not in preserving it. To my knowledge, no "civil rights" or anarchist group even claims to be crusading to get "constitutional rights." Conversely, no "reactionary," "bigot, "segregationist or other member of our constitutional underground is trying to deny to any individual or group, his or its rights guaranteed under the Constitution. So the positions occupied by Dr. Douglass and the "rights" and leftist groups are essentially opposite.

In the second place, Dr. Douglass is not "disobeying" the law, but testing the law. And that is in the finest American Tradition. He is neither asking nor intimating that others join him in a "tax-in." His is no incipient Boston Tea Party operation, although it could be said that that, too, would be in the finest American Tradition. "Rebellion to tyrants is obedience to God."

At what point then is rebellion desirable? At what point is it right to break laws? Is it after they collect our firearms, for instance? Or, is the time to buy a gun when it becomes unlawful to own one? Stanley Yankus, an American farmer who defied the government by planting grain on his own land to feed his own cattle, had his farm confiscated. He moved to Australia. Is _that_ the answer?

One answer, certainly, is the Liberty Amendment, which would repeal the Sixteenth Amendment (income tax). Dr. Douglass' "test" should give added impetus to passage of the Liberty Amendment. In addition to the Liberty Amendment, perhaps we should have a constitutional amendment which would bring back the public whipping post for any rich politician who gives away _your_ money.

Or, maybe we ought to restrict the right to vote to those who receive no government check --federal, state, or local After all, we don't let people on trial vote with the jury.

Breaker of more "bad laws" than Martin Luther King or any other Civil Rights Leader is President Lyndon Johnson. And I am not referring to such things as driving an automobile at high speed with a beer can in his hand. I am talking about laws against helping the enemy, and also laws against helping nations which help enemy nations. President Johnson and the State Department deliberately break those laws daily.

The Constitution of the United States does not in any way condone taking it from the "haves" and giving it to the "have-nots." Shall we abide by the Constitution or shall we abide by unconstitutional laws made by a tyrannical majority?

In Socialist America today, one-fourth of the people are already living off of the other three-fourths, completely or partially. In Federalized America, 48 million people now get regular government checks. That's roughly--and it is rough on those of us who pay the bills and don't get any--one out of every two households in America, assuming no duplications. That's even rough on the Post Office, having to deliver them. I dreamed awhile back that our collectivists had an answer for that too: That they plan to integrate carrier pigeons with woodpeckers, forming a Pigeonpecker Corps. The Pigeonpeckers would not only be able to deliver the 48 million government checks, but they would knock on the door when they got there.

Our Foreign Aid has been the lifeblood of Communism, has redistributed our wealth, eaten up our gold reserve, provided free, the world vacations for Congressmen and their families and girlfriends, for Communists, for businessmen trading against our country, and as sorted other enemies.

When Greece was under a government unfriendly to us, we sent 2,200 dress suits to undertakers in Greece. (They'll be the last ones to let us down, no doubt). And now that Greece is under a government friendly to us, we have cut off practically all aid.

We give wheat and Metrecal, bubble-gum and false teeth, birth control equipment and sex rejuvenators. Take your choice. "From each according to his abilities, to each according to his needs."

This confiscation by our government is not only illegal but unchristian. Jesus was not a Socialist. Jesus believed in the profit motive. He recognized that free men had different talents and abilities varying degrees. Some gained more talents than what they had, and these were rewarded with more talents. However, Jesus took away the one talent of the man who did nothing and gave it to the man who had ten talents. He congratulated those who profited.

Private property is hallowed by both the Christian and Jewish religions. Thou shall not steal, or even covet anything that is thy neighbor's! Christ time and again taught the sanctity of property rights. In Matthew 20:15, Jesus asked: "Is it not lawful for me to do what l will with mine own?" Maybe it is in Heaven, but not in the Great Society. Property rights are the sacred foundation of Human Rights.

Where there is erosion of national morality, property rights are always destroyed. Property rights are the foundation of morality. That's the reason one of the Ten Commandments decrees: "Thou shall not steal." The politician who will steal _for_ you will also steal _from_ you. Appealing to our collectivist leaders to save morality is like appealing to the Jesuits to save Unitarianism. The collectivist program is one debt, one nation, one citizenship, one church and one firing squad.

In the midnight of our intoxication few consider the inevitable hang over. Books like this one should help sober all who read it. Finally, one-man, one-vote becomes <u>One Man</u>. Yet no Dictator is as dangerous as the undisciplined desires of the people. Dictators are far more easily done away with. Of all forms of government, a Republic is the least reprehensible; and a tyrannical democracy is the most unbearable. A government which allows the "have-not" majority to confiscate the "excess" earnings and assets of the "have" minority is a governmental tyranny regardless of whether it has free elections or not. For no dictatorship is more corrupt or tyrannical than the dictatorship of the mob.

Most opponents of higher taxes merely engage in ineffectual foot dragging operations trying to prevent government from taking more. Dr. Douglass, instead, gets to the root of the problem. His argument is not that the income tax should be <u>less</u> but that the income tax is <u>illegal</u>. Thus Dr. Douglass instead of attacking the monkey, attacks the organ grinder. More power--untaxed power--to Dr. Douglass! History is made not by majorities but by dedicated minorities and courageous patriots like Dr. Douglass. Whether freedom continues to ring for us depend on whether the dedicated Douglasses and others who stand up for what is right are more powerful and effective than the dedicated minority for evil which delivered us to the brink.

Tom Anderson

Nashville, Tennessee
1968

IRS Director
Warns Taxpayers

Letter to the Editor:

From time to time, particularly during the tax filing period, a few individuals make public statements expressing their views about Federal Income Taxes. We are most fortunate to live in a country whose constitution guarantees the privilege of freedom of speech. It is unfortunate, however, when a few individuals in exercising this right make statements which can be misleading and' if not carefully examined, might persuade people to lose confidence in the administration of public laws, including our Federal Tax laws.

Some individuals are heard to say that they neither file a return nor pay income taxes and in fact encourage others to do likewise. Others say they file an income tax return but do not include their tax payment. Actually these individuals do pay the full tax for which they are liable and the public should know that they do. However, because of the strict statutory provisions which rightfully protect the tax matters of an individual from disclosure, individual cases cannot be discussed. People making these statements generally fall into one of the following categories:

(a) Those who do not have sufficient income to incur a tax liability,

(b) Those who pay by means of taxes withheld from their wages, and

(c) Those who do not remit payment with their tax return, but either pay it upon receipt of the first notice of tax due, or include a note stating where the money is on deposit for tax collection.

97% of the income tax in the United States is voluntarily reported and paid. This is a tribute to the integrity and patriotism of the American citizen which is unmatched by any other country in the world. This overwhelming majority who believe in supporting a government which insures their freedom should know that those few individuals who say they feel no such obligation are dealt with firmly and in no way escape the payment of income tax when a tax liability is incurred.

Public confidence in the integrity of our tax system and in equitable enforcement of the tax laws is an invaluable asset that must be protected, preserved and maintained. In order that the hundreds of thousands of conscientious taxpayers in our Cincinnati District will not be misled by the statements of a few, I want to assure them that we in IRS are dedicated to administer and enforce the Federal Tax laws in such a manner as to merit their confidence and respect.

Paul A. Schuster
District Director
Cincinnati, Ohio

WILLIAM CAMPBELL DOUGLASS, MD
GENERAL PRACTICE
1812 Hillview Street
Sarasota, Florida

APRIL, 15 1966

Mr. Henry Fowler
Secretary of the U. S. Treasury
Washington 25, D. C.

Dear Mr. Secretary:

Never before in the history of any nation has there been such tolerance and accommodation of treason as now exists in the United States--history shows no parallel. Because the United States Government is now, for all practical purposes, controlled by the Communist conspiracy, I must for moral, religious and Constitutional reasons refuse to pay any further federal income tax. Cicero said in 54 B.C., "We are taxed in our bread and our wine, in our income and our investments, in our land and on our property, not only for base creatures who do not deserve the name of men, but for foreign nations..." Cicero could have been speaking for us as well.

Many high officials in the United States Government, both elected And un-elected, are guilty of violating multiple sections of the United States Criminal Code including Sections 241, 371, 1001, 2382, 2384, and 2385. They are also guilty of violating Section 4.21 of the Internal Revenue Agents Training Manual and Sections 7214 and 7623, Title 26, Internal Revenue Code. These same officials are guilty of violating the 4th, 5th, 6th, 7th, 14th, and 16th Amendments of the United States Constitution.

As a result of these multiple criminal acts, many billions of dollars of income taxes have been used to further a Communist state in the United States. Over a million industrial, labor, education, trade and other types of organizations and corporations have functioned under a system of administrative law which is identical to Communist law as practiced in Russia and its satellites. These organizations have evaded billions and billions of dollars in Federal income taxes and these unpaid taxes have been made up by the docile serfs in this nation known as the middle class taxpayer. The taxes collected from America's working citizens have been the basic wellspring from which Communists and Communist collaborators have worked to destroy completely the free enterprise system in the United States and to set up a Communist government in the United States. The domestic Communist Conspiracy and the International Communist Conspiracy are financed almost completely, and of course involuntarily, by the America taxpayer. The United States Government has allowed foundations, labor unions, tax-exempt organizations and others, through the use of tax free money, to destroy the very fabric of our nation and set up what is essentially a Communist police state varying little from that in Russia today or that of Hitler's socialist dictatorship.

As young American soldiers die in Viet Nam, the tax money of the American people is being used to supply food, guns and ammunition to the enemies of these American sons. Recently Yugoslavia, for instance, received five million dollars worth of copper scrap which is essential to the Communist conquest of America. Yugoslavia also received three million dollars worth of raw material needed to manufacture rayon cord which is used for military truck tires. Communist countries, dedicated to the burial of the United States, have received two and one-half million dollars worth of grinding machines necessary for the manufacture of rocket launchers, bazookas, rifles and cannon barrels. Wheat in vast quantities has been sold to all Communist countries, including Soviet Russia, for the manufacture of industrial alcohol which is necessary for the manufacture of ammunition and fuels for rockets and jet aircraft. How can any Christian allow the Federal Government to force him into committing murder against fellow Americans through this treasonous supplying of war material to the enemy? (See Article 3, Section 3 of the United States Constitution.)

In giving aid and comfort to the enemies of the United States, the United States Government is committing treason against the American people. Those who control the levers of governmental power cannot and will not force me to commit treason against my country, my family, my friends and myself.

The 10th Amendment of the Constitution of the United States says, "The powers not delegated to the United States by the Constitution nor prohibited by it to the States are reserved to the States respectively or to the people." It follows then that all foreign aid is unconstitutional as the Federal Government does not have the legal right to make gifts of American tax money to foreigners. Foreign aid to our enemies is not only unconstitutional; it is immoral and treasonous. I offer the following documentation as evidence that elected and non-elected representatives of the Federal Government are giving aid and comfort to the enemies of these United States and are therefore guilty of treason:

2

1. Communist Indonesia (under the leadership of Sukamo the Japanese collaborator and Vicious Communist murderer of tens of thousands): nine hundred and thirty-eight million dollars in aid which has enabled Sukamo to keep one hundred million Indonesians under slavery.

2. Communist Yugoslavia (under the iron rule of the vicious Communist beast Tito): two billion, five hundred eighty-six million dollars in American tax money to enable Tito to keep 19 million Yugoslavians under slavery.

3. Communist Russia (the fountainhead of the Anti-Christ which is about to take over the entire world in the process of which 60 million Americans are to be murdered--they have openly admitted this): one hundred eighty-six million dollars. This, of course does not include the billions of dollars given to them in World War II.

4. Communist Poland (under the iron-fisted rule of Communist puppet Gomulka): five hundred and forty-eight million American tax dollar to enable Gomulka and his henchmen to keep 30 million Poles under Communist slavery.

5. Communist Cuba (under the rule of one of the most vicious assassins in all history, Fidel Castro): fifty-two million dollars has been received in aid and, as recently as 1965, two hundred and thirty thousand dollars in American tax dollars were given to Castro through a Communist front known as UNICEF. Americans have even been forced into paying the lion's share of the Communism spy school in Cuba (documentation supplied on request). Seven million Cubans are being held in slavery and under sub-human living conditions partially with the help of, American tax dollars.

6. Algeria (under the rule of Ben Bella until he was replaced by an other Communist): one hundred forty-nine million tax dollars which have been and are being used to keep eleven million Algerians in slavery.

7. Communist satellite Burma: one hundred and ten million dollars.

8. Communist Ghana (under the dictatorship of the Communist Kwame Nkrumah): one hundred and sixty-three million tax dollars which are used by the Russians to further communize Africa. Even the Marxist oriented, but

ostensibly anticommunist, Senator Dodd said that Ghana was Russia's first satellite in Africa. Yet, the America people who are looked upon by arrogant bureaucrats at stupid and servile worms, are expected to take this treason indefinitely. This citizen will take it no longer.

The 16th Amendment to the United States Constitution is being administered unconstitutionally because the tax is not levied equally on all citizens. The Constitution of the (United States specifically states that all taxes must be levied equally,(see United States Constitution Article 1, Section 8). The 16th Amendment was not passed to enable the Internal Revenue Service to set up a Gestapo that grants tax favoritism to enemies of the people. It was not set up to be a collection agency for Soviet Russia. The Internal Revenue Service has become an international revenue service primarily for the benefit of the enemies of these United States. It is now obvious that there is an interlocking conspiracy between the Internal Revenue

Service, the various departments of government, large corporations, tax exempt foundations and unions to harass and destroy those American citizens who obstruct the progress of the Bolshevik state in America. These various groups and agencies use the IRS to blacklist, boycott, harass, intimidate, persecute and destroy many Americans who only wish to be left alone and abide by the Constitution of the United States as it was written and intended to be enforced. No American who loves his country and is concerned about the welfare of his family can any longer allow his tax monies to be used to finance this intergovernmental conspiracy which is liquidating the Constitution of the United States, disarming us before our common enemies, while at the same time arming our enemies through the use of tax monies, subverting the morality and decency of the people, openly condoning and often encouraging sedition and treason, and very rapidly confiscating all of the assets of the American people. I was born a Christian and raised a Christian and I therefore adhere to the Christian tenet that it is a sin to commit suicide. Financing my own enemies is suicide. I cannot allow the Federal Government to force me to pay taxes in order to take my own life.

The Federal Government and the IRS have been viciously unfair in the administration of the tax laws. The favored few have paid little or no taxes while the majority have been ground down and oppressed with their own money. The following tax evaders, for instance, have never been brought to justice: Adam Clayton

Powell; Vice President Alben Barkley, (he didn't even bother to file); Dwight David Eisenhower, (a tax evader on a grand scale), and Billy Sol Estes.

Tax-exempt subversive organizations, hiding behind the protective mantle of the Federal Government, are riding herd on the American people. Through the device of tax exemption, the American people are being forced indirectly to subsidize organizations dedicated to the destruction of the United States. The Tax-Exempt Division of the Internal Revenue Service has issued tens of thousands of non-audited and non-supervised letters of exemption to various tax exempt organizations that are working assiduously to brainwash the American people into accepting Bolshevism and hating Americanism. This insidious cabal has reached gigantic proportions and tens of thousands of organizations are affiliated with this conspiracy,

One example of this treason by tax-exempt foundations is the Institute of Pacific Relations. The Carnegie Corporation, the Carnegie Endowment for International Peace (which is actually a very war-like organization in spite of its name)and the Rockefeller Foundation contributed millions of dollars to this organization. The Institute of Pacific Relations was proven, by the government itself, to be a vast and highly effective and very lethal Communist espionage ring. The extent to which the Marxist tax-exempt foundations in the United States are financing the Communist conspiracy is not known because it has never been satisfactorily investigated. The Reece Committee investigated tax-exempt foundations, but they were only able to scratch the surface, because of pro-Communists within the government not allowing them to have enough funds to properly investigate this conspiracy.

Another example of blatant government support of subversive groups is the Metropolitan Music School incorporated. This "corporation" is a government-cited Communist organization yet it has tax exemption. Another is the Highlander Folk School, now called the Highlander Center. This is a purely Communist race-hating group and its parent body, the Highlander Folk Center, has been officially cited by the government as a Communist front. The NAACP ,CORE, SNCC and all the other race-hating, Communist-dominated organizations pay no income tax and are therefore indirectly subsidized by the long-suffering American taxpayer.

The National Science Foundation gave forty-nine hundred dollars to Gaylord Guy King who is head of the Indiana University Chapter of the W. E. B. DuBois Club -- a government-cited Communist organization. (See Attorney General's list of subversive organizations.) The National Science Foundation of Indiana University has been guilty of other treasonable activities, (see report of Congressman Rodabush).

Many departments of our Federal Government are now openly or covertly controlled by the Communist conspiracy. An example is the United States Post Office, which cooperates very closely with the Central Intelligence Agency and the IRS in harassing and intimidating American citizens. As evidence of the fact that the United States Post Office is now basically Communist-controlled, one needs only look at the distribution in the United States of tons and tons of Communist propaganda from Soviet countries at no cost to the Soviets. All of this subversive material is paid for, through force, by the American taxpayer.

Another example of essential Communist control is the U. S. Commerce Department. While our forces in Viet Nam are fighting with defective ammunition and other worn out equipment, the Commerce Department of the United States is encouraging American businessmen to ship billions and billions of dollars of war material to our enemies. Copper, polystyrene, wheat, entire manufacturing plants such as steel mills, fertilizer plants, various chemicals needed in the production of war materials, and spare parts for their war machinery are all shipped to our enemy through the connivance and encouragement of the United States Department of Commerce. Certainly paying taxes to such a government is morally indefensible. The Central Intelligence Agency has now become, if it was not always, the American arm of the Russian NKVD. Even Khrushchev himself has bragged that he knows what is going on in the CIA almost before it is planned. Castro was put in power in Cuba through the connivance of the CIA and the only strong anti-Communist leader in the Dominican Republic, General Wesson Y. Wesson, was kidnapped by our Central Intelligence Agency. Castro is kept in power by the CIA which keeps the Cuban Freedom Fighters in South Florida constantly off balance, harassed, and confused. Not even the American Congress is allowed to know how many tax dollars are poured into this subversive organization. Admiral Hillenkoetter, former head of the Central Intelligence Agency, has admitted that the CIA is full of Communist spies--and he was not able to do anything about it.

Another example of blatant Communism in action in the United States is Lyndon Johnson's War on Poverty. This is truly a war against the middle class American citizen. Teachers, who have taken part in this program have been brainwashed with Communist books by such noted Communists as Woody Guthrie, Howard Fast, W. E. B. DuBois, Ann Braden and Herbert Aptheker. Many of these so named are top functionaries in the Communist party which is dedicated to the overthrow of the United States. Yet, their works are recommended by Lyndon Johnson's War on Poverty Commissars. Poverty funds have been given to Bolshevik racist fanatics in New York City; funds have been used to support prostitution and in many other ways the money is being used to subvert the morals and the morale of America's youth.

The Department of State has become, for all practical purposes, a branch of the Russian Embassy taking its orders primarily from New York City, (the United Nations). The United States Department is today entirely under the direction of our Bolshevik enemy. This is true beyond a shadow of a doubt and in evidence I offer the following documentation to wit:

Secretary of State Dean Rusk is himself a very serious security risk. Rusk has been a Communist collaborator all of his adult life. By. 1946 Mr. Rusk had a very active file with our Intelligence Services due to his strong pro-Communist sympathies and activities. In spite of this, in 1946 he was appointed Chief of Internal Security Affairs of the Department of State. In March of 1947 he replaced the spy Alger Hiss as Director of Special Political Affairs. Rusk continued the policies of the spy Alger Hiss in cooperating closely with the Communist conspiracy by keeping known Communists and other security risks in the State Department and filling jobs in the United Nations with these traitors. Alger Hiss and Dean Rusk were responsible for at least 26 American Communists getting key jobs in the United Nations. There can be no question that Spy Hiss, and his Communist collaborator Rusk, knew that these men were Communist espionage agents as their files, containing this information, were in the State Department at the time they were hired. Although Mao Tse Tung had murdered tens of millions of Chinese, Dean Rusk called him "The George Washington of China". Dean Rusk was responsible for the United States rejecting Chiang Kai-shek's offer of troops in Korea and so Rusk was indirectly responsible for the death of many Americans in the Korean war. It was Dean Rusk who formulated the plan to not win in Korea, who tied General MacArthur's hands and who finally was responsible for General MacArthur's being removed from Command. Dean Rusk recommended a two million dollar grant to the Institute of Pacific Relations from the pro-Communist institution known as the Rockefeller Foundation. As reported above, the Institute of Pacific Relations was found to be a Communist espionage ring. (M. Rusk was a member of this Communist espionage ring). This is only a brief sketch of the Communist collaborator Dean Rusk. More information and documentation will be supplied on request.

James Harland Cleveland, Assistant Secretary of State for International Affairs: This man has a long history of Communist associations. He has written for a number of Communist magazines. Cleveland recently tried to slip the traitor Alger Hiss back into the government. Mr. Cleveland's record is long and sordid and documentation and witnesses will be supplied on request.

Wilbur J. Cohen, Assistant Secretary of the Department of Health, Education and Welfare: Long history of association with Communists and Communist sympathizers. Wilbur Cohen has many Communist affiliations documentation supplied on request.

Harry Conover, Councilor U. S. Embassy Buenos Aires: A long and involved Communist record -- documentation supplied on request.

Daniel Margolies, Supervisor of International Relations Office: This man has associated with many known Communists and has a number of Communist front affiliations --documentation and witnesses supplied on request.

Livingston Merchant: A long and notorious record of associations with Communists and Communist agents. He was reported reliably as being a member of a group in the State Department completely under the control of Soviet Intelligence.

Alexander L. Peaslee, Chief of the Asian Communist Areas Division in the Bureau of Intelligence and Research Department of State: This man and his wife have been reported by our Intelligence Services as being a contact of Soviet Intelligence who were supplying confidential and secret information to the enemy. Documentation supplied on request.

David H. Popper, Director, Office of Atlantic Political and Military Affairs, Department of State: A friend of many Communist agents and on the editorial board of the subversive magazine Amerasia--documentation supplied on request.

Hugh C. Reichard, formerly in the Intelligence Research Division of the State Department, now in International Relations Office: Many Communist associations and a draft dodger--documentation supplied on request.

J. J. Reinstein U. S. Embassy Paris: Close friend of identified Communist agent Donald Hiss (brother of Alger Hiss now working for former Secretary of State, Dean Acheson--himself a Communist collaborator) .

Walt Whitman Rostow: This man is such a serious security risk that when he was considered for a high post in the United States Air Force he was rejected. Documentation supplied on request.

Abba Schwartz, Administrator, Bureau of Security and Councilor Affairs: A friend of a number of Communists, Soviet agents and homosexuals. This man is responsible for many Communist spies coming from Red China and Cuba into the United States at the expense of the American taxpayer. He was responsible for the return of one Lee Harvey Oswald to Russia where he trained to kill the President of the United States. Abba Schwartz stole the file on Lee Harvey Oswald after Oswald shot the President. No action has been taken against him for this malfeasance in office.

John Stewart Service: Reported as an espionage agent. He was given a loyalty clearance by a personnel board in the State Department consisting of Selden Chapman, Nelson Rockefeller, Dean Acheson, Julius Holmes. This case has been suppressed according to an affidavit by a court reporter--documentation and witnesses supplied on request.

Julian Singman, known to live with homosexuals and also a close friend of Adlai Stevenson and Abba Schwartz. A serious security risk.

Charles N. Spinks, State Department employee detached to U. S. Information Agency: Spinks was a dues-paying member of the espionage ring known as the Institute of Pacific Relations and wrote for their Communist magazine Pacific Affairs. Spinks has many Communist friends including espionage agent Thomas A. Bission, Communist collaborator Michael Greenberg, Andrew Roth, and Emmanuel S. Larson.

In spite of his highly subversive background, Spinks has been assigned to top secret intelligence work. Documentation and witnesses supplied on request.

Edward A. Symans, now retired at taxpayers expense: Named by a Soviet defector as a Soviet espionage agent for 18 years while in government service. In spite of this Symans was allowed to resign. He was then re-hired and pensioned off at taxpayers expense. The name Symans is an alias. His real name is Symansky. I will not pay one jot of this traitor 's retirement.

Dr. Phillip Talbot, Assistant Secretary of State: This man has a long history of association with Communists an Communist sympathizers and Soviet agents. He was a dues-paying member of the espionage ring known as the Institute of Pacific Relations -- documentation and witnesses supplied on request.

Leonard Unger, U. S. Ambassador to Laos: Unger is one of the group in the State Department constituting a suspected espionage ring. Security officer Scott McCloud considered Unger a security risk as far back as 1956. Unger has a long list of Communist associations and affiliations--documentation and witnesses supplied on request.

William Wieland, alias Montenegro: A key figure in the downfall of Cuba and its take over by Communist Castro. Wieland has long been known as a serious security risk and he is now helping to subvert Australia at the expense of the American taxpayer. Documentation and witnesses supplied on request.

Adam Yarmolinsky, Special Assistant to the Secretary of Defense: Yarmolinsky and his family have had a long association with Communists, Communist agents and other subverters of the American way. His sordid background is too long and involved to document here but documentation and witnesses will be supplied on request.

This is a very brief sample of the spies and traitors in the Department of State at the present time. There are hundreds of others and documentation and witnesses will be supplied on request.

The following persons and departments are also involved in the conspiracy:

Mrs. Esther Peterson, Assistant Secretary of Labor. Mrs. Peterson and her husband have been long-time security risks and were close friends and contacts with identified Communist John Abt, identified Communist Charles Krivitsky, identified Communist Victor Perlo and identified Communist Lee Pressman. The pro-Communist background of this Assistant Secretary of Labor is long and involved and documentation and witnesses will be supplied on request.

The President of the United States, Lyndon Baines Johnson: The Communist Party, under the direction of Mr. Gus Hall, openly endorsed Lyndon Baines Johnson and the Democratic Party for re-election in 1964. Communists the world over went all out for the re-election of Lyndon B. Johnson for the Presidency. Hubert Humphrey, Vice President of the United States, has also shown himself to be completely acceptable to the international Communist conspiracy.

The United States Supreme Court: The United States Supreme Court has become one of the most important instruments of Communist global conquest. On November 15, 1965, the United States Supreme Court gave domestic Communists complete constitutional protection by ruling that members of the Communist Party no longer have to register as agents of a foreign power. The Communists themselves have openly admitted that this is the greatest victory in their history. The Supreme Court has handicapped the police and the FBI. It has usurped the powers of Congress and destroyed the security of these United States.

Chief Justice Earl Warren, a close friend of the Communist butcher Tito, has gone all out for complete surrender of American sovereignty to a world body. This is a direct violation of his oath to support and defend the Constitution of the United States. (See also Public Law 85766, Section 1602). He votes consistently for the Communists in cases before the Supreme Court.

Hugo Black Associate Justice of the Supreme Court: Mr. Black, a former member of the Ku Klux Klan, has been associated with Communist front organizations (see HCUA appendix 9, page 1581). His voting record is 100% pro-Communist.

William O. Douglas Associate Justice: Justice Douglas has a long line of Communist affiliations. He has voted 97% pro--communist.

Justice Brennan has close to a 100% pro-Communist voting record.

11

Abe Fortas, Associate Justice: A defender of Communists and a member of many Communist front organizations including the National Lawyers Guild and the Southern Conference for Human Welfare.

A convicted traitor, George J. Gessner, has been set free on a fantastically asinine technicality. In any country with the government responsible to the welfare and safety of the citizenry, Gessner would have been executed. The Federal Judge in this case is still receiving a paycheck from the American taxpayer.

Many members of the United States Senate and the House of Representatives have records of Communist affiliations and Communist associations. The list is too long and involved to enumerate here but details will be supplied on request. Examples of members of the United States Senate with Communist affiliations and associations are Senators Gruening, Javits, Douglas and Saltonstall. The records of Gruening, Douglas and Saltonstall can be found in the investigations of the House Committee on Un-American Activities of 1944 (Appendix 9).

Certain senators, who are supporting Senate Concurrent Resolution No. 32 are in violation of their oath of office to support and defend the Constitution of the United States. This Concurrent Resolution calls for the establishing of an international police force and a disarmament organization through a new United Nations treaty. The Resolution also calls for financial support of this disarmament organization and international police force. Anyone who supports disarmament of the United States cannot at the same time claim to be fulfilling his oath to support and defend the United States.

These Senators are also in violation of Public Law 85766, Section 1602 which states: "No part of the funds appropriated in this or any other Act shall be used to pay... any person, firm or corporation, or any combination of persons, firms or corporations, to conduct a study or plan when or how or in what circumstances the Government of the United States should surrender this country and its people to any foreign power..."

The following Senators, whose salaries are paid by the U. S. taxpayers, are supporting the above mentioned treasonous Concurrent Resolution No. 32: Senators McGovern, Bayh, Church, Bartlett, Burdick, Brewster, Mondale, Hart, Inoye, Javits, Long

(Mo.), McGee, Morse, Moss, Newberger, Pell, Proxmire, Randolph, Tydings, Williams (N. J.),Young (Ohio).

The United Nations: Section 109, Public Law 471 states: "It is illegal to use funds for any project that promotes One World Government or One World Citizenship." The United Nations, designed by Communist Alger Hiss and other traitors, is the Communist instrument by which the sovereignty of the United States is being transferred to an international Communist-controlled government. It is therefore natural that most of the Americans in key positions in the United Nations would be Americans in name only.

The American Ambassador to the United Nations Arthur Goldberg: has a long history of Communist collaboration and Communist sympathies.

Mr. Ralph Bunch, Under Secretary General of the United Nation, and therefore one or the three most influential men in that organization, is a dedicated world Marxist. Mr. Bunch has been declared a serious security risk on the floor of the United States House of Representatives. His pro-Communist record is long and easily documented and this documentation will be supplied on request.

Mr. Philip Jessup: "Our" Representative on the World Court, was considered such a serious security risk by the United States Senate that he was disapproved as United States delegate to the United Nations in 1951.

The United States taxpayers pay the lion share of the expenses of the United Nations which is being used to destroy our nation and kill off all of our youth in foreign wars. It is now well known that both sides of the Korean War were controlled from the United Nations by Russian General Constantine Zinchenko. The present bloodletting operation in Vietnam is also controlled by the Communists through the United Nations. General Westmoreland, the figurehead commander of our troops, (and himself a member of the Communist-collaborating Council on Foreign Relations) is under command of Russian General Vladimir Suslove from the U.N. It is, of course, impossible for America to win a war when its troops are commanded by the enemy, This undoubtedly will go down in history as the most colossal fraud and sham of all time. No American who does not classify himself as a Communist-collaborator can allow his money to be spent on this mass murder of young American citizens.

The Solicitor General of the U.S., <u>Thurgood Marshall, the top trial lawyer in these United States</u>, is sympathetic to the Communist cause an was an <u>officer</u> in a Communist organization (see HCUA appendix 9, page 795). This pro-Communist racist fanatic once said, "I want you to understand that when the colored people take over, every time a white man draws a breath he will have to pay a fine." I cannot, with a clear conscience, pay one infinitesimal portion of this creature's salary and I refuse to do so. (Now a Supreme Court Justice--Ed.)

<u>Robert C. Weaver, Secretary, Department of Housing and Urban Development</u>, has a shameful record of cooperation with the Communist enemy. His pro-Communist and Communist associations are: Negro Peoples Committee (see HCUA Appendix 9. Page 184), and Washington Book Shop (see letter by Attorney General Clark, December 4,1947 and September 21,1948). I will not be forced to pay one penny of tribute to a government that promotes rather than hangs collaborators such as Robert C. Weaver.

Treason, anarchy and sedition have become rampant within these United States. Herbert Aptheker, Communist; Staughton Lynd, Marxist fanatic and Thomas Hayden, anti-American revolutionary, have all been in violation of the Immigration and Nationality Acts of 1952. For conniving with the enemy they are each subject to a $5,000 fine and 5 years in a Federal penitentiary. They are also in violation of the Logan Act. These three traitors traveled to North Vietnam, without benefit of passports, to deal with the Red butcher of North Vietnam, Ho Chi Minh. What instructions did these enemies of America receive from their master in Hanoi? Were their instructions similar to those received by one Lee Harvey Oswald when he made his sojourn to Mexico? The President of the United States, the Attorney General and the State Department, apparently in collusion with these traitors, remain silent. I will not pay the salaries of men who collaborate with my country's enemies. Many other examples of sedition and treason, carried on with the tacit approval of the Johnson administration, will be supplied on request.

If you wish further evidence that the United States is controlled for all practical purposes, by the Communist enemy, or if you wish the names of more individuals who have avoided millions of dollars in taxes, I will supply them on request.

Sincerely yours,
William Campbell Douglass, MD

14

IN THE DISTRICT COURT OF THE UNITED STATES
FOR THE MIDDLE DISTRICT OF FLOR1DA
TAMPA DIVISlON

UNITED STATES OF AMERICA : and BLAKELY I. DAVIS, Internal Revenue Agent, Petitioners, -vs- WILLIAM C. DOUGLASS, Respondent.	No. 66-426-Civil T

Tampa, Florida
Tuesday, December 13,1966

The above entitled cause came onforhearing, pursuant to Amended Order to Show Cause, before the Honorable Joseph P. Lieb, United States District Judge, in Chambers, at Tampa, Florida, on Tuesday, December 13, 1966, commencing at 1:15 o'clock p.m.

APPEARANCES:

STEPHEN FUERTH, ESQ., Department of Justice, Tax Division Washington, D.C.;

-and-

THOMAS G. WILSON, ESQ., United States Attorney's Office, Tampa, Florida; appearing on behalf of Petitioners.

WILLIAM C. DOUGLASS, MD, 1812 Hillview Street, Sarasota, Florida; appearing on his own behalf as Respondent.

ALSO PRESENT:

BLAKELY I. DAVIS, Internal Revenue Agent, a Petitioner.

LARRY SIDES, a friend and intervenor for the Respondent.

15

UNITED STATES DISTRICT COURT
MIDDLE DISTRICT OF FLORIDA
TAMPA DIVISION

UNITED STATES OF AMERICA and
BLAKELY I. DAVIS, Internal
Revenue Agent,

        Petitioners,

vs.

WILLIAM C. DOUGLASS,

        Respondent.

No. 66-426 Civ. T.

AMENDED ORDER TO SHOW CAUSE

Upon the petition, the exhibits attached thereto, the affidavit of Blakely I. Davis, Internal Revenue Agent, and upon the motion of Edward F. Boardman, United States Attorney for the middle District of Florida.

IT IS ORDERED that William C. Douglass appear before the District Court of the United States for the Middle District of Florida, in that branch thereof presided over by the under-signed in his courtroom in the United States Courthouse in Tampa, Florida, on December 13, 1966, at 1:15 p.m. to show cause why he should not be compelled to testify and produce the records demanded in the Internal Revenue Service summons served upon him on August 30, 1966, by the petitioner, Blakely I. Davis.

LET A COPY OF THIS ORDER together with the petition and the exhibits attached thereto, be mailed to the said respondent at least five (5) days prior to the time set herein for hearing.

Entered at Tampa, Florida, this _____ day of December, 1966.

Joseph P. Lieb

UNITED STATES DISTRICT JUDGE

THE COURT: Dr. Douglass, do you have an attorney?

DR. DOUGLASS: No, sir, I do not.

MR. WILSON: Your Honor, Mr. Fuerth is present from the Department of Justice.

THE COURT: You understand, Dr. Douglass, that the gentleman that spoke to me, Mr. Wilson, is an Assistant District Attorney. And you are --

MR. FUERTH: I am an attorney with the Department of Justice Tax Division.

THE COURT: Dr. Douglass says he has no attorney, so he is appearing for himself. This is a matter in a case involving the United State and Dr. Douglass. It is Case No. 66-426-Civil Tampa. The matter arises out of the relations between Dr. Douglass and an agent of the Internal Revenue Service, whereby the Internal Revenue Service conducted an investigation and asked Dr. Douglass to produce certain records, and he declined to do so. The United States petitioned to this Court for an order requiring Dr. Douglass to show cause why he refuse: to testify and why he should not be compelled to testify and produce the records demanded.

Now, I don't believe there has been any paper filed, had there Dr. Douglass?

DR. DOUGLASS : What do you mean by "paper", Judge? I am not --

THE COURT: Well, a lawyer would understand it.

DR. DOUGLASS: Yes, sir.

THE COURT: Usually, when there is an order to show cause or response to be made, they usually file a paper, you know, it is in writing. But you didn't have that. I am not too much worried about it. What we are concerned with is what is your reason that you should give now in response to this order to give reasons, to show cause. What is the matter here? What happened?

DR. DOUGLASS: Well, I have an order to show cause here that was presented to me. Is that what you mean?

THE COURT: You have the order to show cause?

DR. DOUGLASS: Yes, sir.

THE COURT: And you are here today to show cause. Now, what I am not trying to pursue this as if you were a lawyer, Doctor. I am trying to pursue as if we could get some mutual understanding. All want to know is, why is it, or do you still decline to produce these records that they want? Do you know what they are after?

DR. DOUGLASS: Yes, sir, I believe I do.

18

THE COURT: Are they taking advantage of you, or are you misunderstanding their objectives or what they are trying to do?

DR. DOUGLASS: No, I don't think I misunderstand their objectives, Judge.

THE COURT: It is a common thing to ask people to produce records. They have done it to me, and I suppose that many, many people have been asked by these agents in the course of their duties to produce certain records. And now I want to know --there is no doubt that they came and asked you for them, is there?

DR. DOUGLASS: No, sir, there is no doubt that they came unannounced and asked me --

THE COURT: Do you know this man that asked you? Did you know Mr. Davis?

DR. DOUGLASS: Yes, sir. I believe he is here, right there. (Indicating).

THE COURT: He is the one right there in the middle?

DR. DOUGLASS: Yes, sir.

THE COURT: What is the reason you don't want to respond?

DR. DOUGLASS: Well, first let me put this on for the record, if I may, Judge.

THE COURT: That's right.

DR. DOUGLASS: Judge, they have investigated my records three out of the past four years. When I first came back to Sarasota out of the Navy and set up my practice, the Internal Revenue Service, for reasons I think I understand, came into my office and went over my books very thoroughly, although for that particular year I had been in practice only three months. Now, this to me was harassment, because I am involved in many anti-Communist activities which you may or may not be familiar with.

THE COURT: What is that?

DR. DOUGLASS: I say I am involved in many anti-Communist activities that you may or may not be familiar with.

THE COURT: I am not, Doctor. I don't know what you are talking about.

DR. DOUGLASS: When they came back the next year and investigated my records again, I felt this was a clear case of harassment. Now would you like me to explain, sir, what my anti-Communist activities have been? I feel this is very pertinent to the case, I really do.

THE COURT: Go ahead with anything you want to say.

DR. DOUGLASS: I am national president of Let Freedom Ring Incorporated. This is the --if I am speaking too fast, I will be glad to slow down.

MR. WILSON: You won't speak too fast for Mr. Slemp.

DR. DOUGLASS: -- This is the national anti-Communist network. Now, this program is a two-minute telephone tape. The person calls an answering machine, and they get a two-minute anti-Communist and often anti-administration message. We have criticized everyone from the President on down for what we feel is very poor leadership and for downright treason in many cases. Now, the Government has not taken to this lightly, and we have been harassed all along. And we have 120 stations across the country, from Seattle --

THE COURT: Well, now, this investigation, Doctor, is your own personal income tax they are after, isn't it?

DR. DOUGLASS: Yes, sir, but I feel this is related to it.

THE COURT: You brought in this other organization, but --

DR. DOUGLASS: I feel this is one of the reasons I have been harassed by the I.R.S.

THE COURT: It may be, I don't know.

DR. DOUGLASS: We have stations in Seattle, Boston, Miami, Houston, Los Angeles, 10 in New York City, and so forth. It has become quite a large and somewhat influential organization, which is trying to awaken the American people to the dangers of Communism, to the utter folly of the Internal Revenue Service the way it is conducted, the way the money is being used for illegal, unconstitutional, and downright treasonous purposes, such as the government now giving aid and comfort to our enemies openly, and so forth.

So when I came back to Sarasota, as I said, I was investigated after being in practice for three months. I suspected this was harassment. When they came back the next year and did it again, I was convinced that it was harassment. Then they skipped a year and they came back again. So I feel that the I.R.S. has been --

THE COURT: You mean you have been investigated for other years besides '65?

DR. DOUGLASS: Three out of four, yes, sir. And I am not a wealthy man. I am flat broke. And I felt there was no other reason for this, because they cleared me the first year, they cleared me the second year, and they came back again. To me this is clearly harassment. But this is not why I refused to show them my books, sir --

THE COURT: That is what I am trying to find out.

DR. DOUGLASS: I thought I should put this in the record, because it is part of the reason I finally got fed up and said I would not pay any more of this tax. Now, the basic reason why I have refused to pay income tax--I wrote "Under Protest" across the form and sent it in signed. I think the best way to explain it, Your Honor--

THE COURT: Let me understand you. From what you said --now, I don it know this case at all, except that they have asked me to bring you in here and to ascertain from you what is your reason for failing to do what they want.

DR. DOUGLASS: Yes, sir.

THE COURT: Do I understand that you volunteer and say that you don't pay any income tax?

DR. DOUGLASS: I am sorry, sir. I don't understand the question.

THE COURT: You said "The reason I don't pay income tax" -- did you mean that? Don't you pay any?

DR. DOUGLASS: I didn't word it that way. The reason I refused to pay income tax this year, this is what I am trying to explain to you, sir, why I wrote "Under Protest" across my Internal Revenue Form 10 --10 whatever it is.

THE COURT: Did you file any return at all?

DR. DOUGLASS: Oh, yes, sir. I filed, yes, sir.

THE COURT: And what does it show that you earned -- nothing?

DR. DOUGLASS: It says "Under Protest". I signed it in blank.

MR. FUERTH: Your Honor, if it is any clarification, I have a copy of that return.

THE COURT: What good is this doing, Doctor? I don't know what you are trying to do here.

DR. DOUGLASS: I think I can best explain it to Your

THE COURT: I can follow you that you feel that you are not being treated courteously or something like that. But you have got sense enough to know that you are supposed to pay income tax if you earn enough; isn't that right?

DR. DOUGLASS: Your Honor, I think the best way to explain this to you is to read certain excerpts from my letter to the Secretary of the Treasury. I wrote him a 17 page letter --

THE COURT: Go ahead. Don't read the whole thing

DR. DOUGLASS: No, sir.

THE COURT. Just tell me what is the reason you don't do it. I see this--I have been handed what purports to be a photostatic copy of a 1040 for 1965, in the name of William C. Douglass, 1812 Hillview, Sarasota, Florida, signed by William C. Douglass, MD. And across the front of it--no boxes have been filled out at all, and there has been hand printed with pen and ink or pencil "Under Protest". That is true, isn't it, Doctor? That is what I have got here.

DR. DOUGLASS: Yes, sir, that's correct.

THE COURT: That is the one you sent in?

DR. DOUGLASS: Yes, sir, that is a copy of it.

THE COURT: That is all I know about it. Now, go ahead.

MR. FUERTH: Your Honor, before we get into this letter, the only thing, I am not aware of any letter that was sent to the Secretary. I wonder if Dr. Douglass -- would Dr. Douglass identify the date of this letter? I do not have a copy of this letter.

THE COURT: I don't know anything about it. I understand all he is trying to do is to tell me an answer to my question, and I am only interested in the answer to one question. Why don't you give these government agents the things that they are asking for? They usually get these things.

DR. DOUGLASS: Yes, sir.

THE COURT: They have a right, as you know, to investigate. We are paying them to investigate. And it calls for a very good reason on your part for failure to cooperate. Now, you understand that. Now, I don't want your letter, I want your explanation.

DR. DOUGLASS: Well, as I said, sir, the best way for me to explain to you -- that is what I want to do is explain to you.

THE COURT: All right. Tell me anything you want, but make it to the point.

DR. DOUGLASS: I won't take a long time, but giving you excerpts from it, I believe, will explain why I have refused to pay income tax for 1965. The first sentence of this letter reads as follows: "Never before in the history of any nation has there been such tolerance and accommodation of treason as now exists in the United States. History, as far as I know, shows no parallel" --

THE COURT: Wait a minute now. Has this got anything to do with your failure to pay your tax?

DR. DOUGLASS: Yes, sir. I think the next sentence will explain it. It is a little more to the point.

THE COURT: All right.

DR. DOUGLASS: (Reading) "Because the United States Government is now for all practical purposes controlled by the Communist conspiracy, I must for moral, religious and constitutional reasons refuse to pay any further income tax." And I am prepared to prove this in a trial by jury. I am prepared to prove that particular sentence.

THE COURT: Is that your reason for declining in the past, and is that your attitude now toward giving the agent the books and records that he has spelled out here in this petition?

DR. DOUGLASS: I have never refused before, Your Honor. This is the first--

22

THE COURT: Well, are you agreeing now to give them, or are you declining to give them?

DR. DOUGLASS: I am declining, sir. -- Unless, of course you order me to.

THE COURT: Well, I am going to order you to, because I don't see any reason why -- I certainly haven't got any sympathy with Communists taking this attitude toward us, and I don't see why I should have a different rule for anti--Communists. I am going to treat them all the same .

DR. DOUGLASS: I haven't really had time, sir, to elaborate the point. One sentence isn't enough to express my point.

THE COURT: It is along the same line, isn't it?

DR. DOUGLASS: Yes. But I can't describe a 17 page letter in one sentence .

THE COURT: You have a notion that you would be cooperating with Communism if you supported the United States Government; is that what you are saying?

DR. DOUGLASS: No, sir. I didn't say that, no, sir.

THE COURT: How did you say it?

DR. DOUGLASS: That I would be cooperating with Communism if I contributed any more money to allow these people to use to support the Communist conspiracy all over the world. And I am prepared to prove that statement, sir.

THE COURT: Well, I don't know how we can -- you can think any- thing you want, Doctor, but the business of the Government is quite far-flung and extensive. Actually, it costs money to maintain the room we are in, and the salaries of the Government officials who are trying to do their work without regard to the difficulties between you and the Communists, and you and the Internal Revenue people, for that matter. I can't allow a person to decline to give the required cooperation just because of the reasons you have given. Now, if you haven't got any- thing else, rest assured that I am going to issue an order against you. I don't want to do it, Doctor. I want you to be just like I am, a willing, cooperative citizen of this country. And this is a good country, as you know, and that is why you are so serious about it.

DR. DOUGLASS: That's correct, sir.

THE COURT: And we can't have -- we can't have a lot of what you might call divergent dissidents around here, whether they be of good intent or bad intent. As I told you a minute ago, I won't let a Communist do what you are trying to do, and I don't see why I should let an anti-Communist do what you are trying to do. People are going to have to comply with the laws of the

Unite as far as I am concerned. Now, if you have a desire to decline even though you are ordered by the Court -- and I think I am fair to you, Doctor -- I think I am fair, and I think you would do the same thing if you were sitting in my job here. I think you would. And I don't want anybody to be misled, I don't want anybody to be unhappy about anything, but the happiest thing around here, I think, would be for you to comply with this, because you just have no right to refuse to pay taxes for the reason you have given. That is not right. Now, what do you want to do?

DR. DOUGLASS: I would like, sir if I maybe allowed, to elaborate a little bit more on why I refused this. The record as it now stands will not show at all, Judge, why --

THE COURT: It will all tend toward the same conclusion?

DR. DOUGLASS: Yes, sir. But in fairness to me, wouldn't it be fairer to me to allow me to put something on the record?

THE COURT: Is it the same, Doctor, it will all tend to show that your sole reason or your premise as you have set it out, that you feel that any money you would contribute would be used for Communist purposes; is that what it is?

DR. DOUGLASS: Not any of it, but a great deal of it, sir. And the record would not be fair, the record would not show -- just making the statement does not give me a chance to really put on the record any true evidence of my position.

THE COURT: Is that the only reason you have?

DR. DOUGLASS: I am a very patriotic American, Your Honor, I believe. I have supported my Government as a member of the Military. Let me ask you this question, Your Honor. If I could prove to you that a large percentage of our income tax monies was being used to support the enemies of our country while Americans are dying in Viet Nam, would you blame me for taking the attitude that I have taken? If I could prove this point, that I would be forced into treason against my own country --

THE COURT: Well, Doctor, I don't know of any way we could have your money divided up so it would only go to the support of the Federal Courts or the Internal Revenue Service, or something, and not some other agency that you may not approve of.

DR. DOUGLASS: Sir, I am prepared to meet that, to prove that a great deal of money is being used for subversive purposes. I am willing to take a jury trial to prove it.

THE COURT: Well, I cannot agree with you that it lies in your power or the power of any taxpayer to decline to pay taxes on the ground that they don't like the way the Government, spends the money. I can't allow that.

DR. DOUGLASS: I wouldn't decline on that ground, sir. I wouldn't decline on the ground that that is basic. Only if the money is being used to destroy me and my family. This is very important to me. If the money is being used to destroy everything in which I believe, sir, I feel it is my duty to refuse to pay it, and I am prepared to prove it, sir, if I am given the opportunity.

THE COURT: I feel there are other ways you could show your disapproval of it--

DR. DOUGLASS: I have tried every way I know.

THE COURT: -- rather than pick out something like this. The people of the United States have allowed you to live in this country and practice and make money, and enjoy the benefits of common citizenship. And the people of the United States are in turn entitled to have you contribute like everybody else.

DR. DOUGLASS: I have contributed every way I know how? sir. I have contributed all my life.

THE COURT: Now, that is all we want to know. Do you want to go along with these agents here, or do you want to do something else?

DR. DOUGLASS: Well, Your Honor, first, as I said before, I would tike to have the opportunity to put a little bit more in my statement.

THE COURT: I will give you an opportunity. Put some more in, Doctor.

DR. DOUGLASS: All right, sir. Thank you.

THE COURT: But you are going to have to show more than just the idea that you have advanced up to now. Go ahead.

DR. DOUGLASS: Shall I continue, sir? "As young Americans die in Viet Nam" -- this is from my letter again -- "the tax money of the American people is being used to supply food, guns and ammunition to enemies of these American sons. Recently, for instance, Yugoslavia received 5,000,000 dollars worth of copper scrap which is essential to the Communist conquest of America. Yugoslavia also received 3,000,000 dollars worth of raw material needed to manufacture rayon cord which is used for military truck tires. Communist countries dedicated to the burial of the United States have received 2,500,000 dollars worth of grinding machines necessary for the manufacture of rocket launchers, bazookas, rifle and cannon barrels. Wheat in vast quantities" -- and I might interject here, we are facing a drastic wheat shortage in this country -- "Wheat in vast quantities has been sold or given to almost every Communist country in the world including Soviet Russia, which says that we are their primary enemy and they are out to destroy us. This was sold to them for the manufacture of industrial alcohol, which is necessary to the manufacture of ammunition and fuels for rockets and jet aircraft. "

I simply do not understand how any Christian can allow the federal Government to force him into committing murder against other Americans through this treasonous supply of war material to the enemy. I have no objection whatsoever to paying taxes for legitimate purposes, because I am a patriotic American. But when I have seen year after year, after 15 years of study, Your Honor, a larger and larger and larger percentage of my money being used to destroy my country, it is time that I do something about it. It is mandatory that I do something about it. And I can't understand why tens of thousands of people haven't risen up in revolt against this. By "revolt", I mean peaceful revolt by refusing to pay any money for their own destruction and the destruction of their own families.

The Tenth Amendment of the Constitution of the United States says -- now, I am no attorney, but I can read the Constitution, and that is the only thing I know about the law, is the Constitution. My knowledge of the law goes no further than that. -- "The powers not delegated to the United States by the Constitution or prohibited by it to the States, are reserved to the States respectively, or to the people." It follows then that all foreign aid is unconstitutional, and certainly foreign aid to our enemy is not only unconstitutional, it is down-right treason. I would like to offer a little documentation for the record as evidence that elected and non-elected representatives of the Federal Government are giving aid and comfort to the enemies of the United States, and are, therefore guilty of treason.

THE COURT: Did it ever occur to you, Doctor, that this country, bad as you may think it is, is still the best place to live?

DR. DOUGLASS: There is no question about that, Your Honor. It is my country, I love it. It is the finest country in the history of the world.

THE COURT: We all have that in common. We are very certain that it is true that this nation, as we have it, is the best place to live and it is much to be preferred over the Communist.

DR. DOUGLASS: Absolutely, sir.

THE COURT: And doesn't it follow that if you let this country fall by not supporting it, the only result will be that this country, too, will also be Communist?

26

DR. DOUGLASS: Yes, sir.

THE COURT: Now, that is what you are heading for here.

DR. DOUGLASS: No, sir, I don't fee I that I am.

THE COURT: Huh?

DR. DOUGLASS: No, sir.

THE COURT: Who is going to defend this country if everybody rises up, as you say, against it?

DR. DOUGLASS: I don't expect everyone to rise up against it, but I don't expect it to survive if the money is being used to support our enemies, sir. And I am prepared to prove that they are doing just exactly this. I am prepared to name individuals in the Government who have long, long pro-Communist records or who are in very sensitive positions and have never been investigated. Something has to be done to bring this to the attention of the American people. I am willing to face a jury trial or whatever to bring this out to the American people, that our country is rapidly being destroyed from the inside, using our own money.

THE COURT: Doctor, you may have the sympathy of everybody that hears you speak and all of that, but we have a problem here that is something else. We have a problem of saving our country.

DR. DOUGLASS: Yes, sir.

THE COURT: And part of this is not only respect for law, but to contribute to the support of the Government, which is --

DR. DOUGLASS: I have the utmost respect for the law, Your Honor.

THE COURT: -- by paying the tax. You haven't made an answer that is a sufficient answer here. That is not so. We can't have that. We can't allow you, Dr. Douglass, nor John Jones nor Pete Smith or anybody else, to come in here and say, "I choose not to pay any tax.. We can't have that. You know that.

DR. DOUGLASS: I am not saying that I choose not to pay, Your Honor.

THE COURT: That is what we are all here for.

DR. DOUGLASS: I merely want to bring this thing to a head to show that the money is being used to destroy us, you as well as me.

THE COURT: You can bring it to a head in some fashion without violating the law.

DR. DOUGLASS: No, sir, I don't want to violate the law.

THE COURT: You have the right to free speech in this country, the right to make your protest in lawful ways. There are many of them. You don't need me to tell you how to do this. You are smart.

DR. DOUGLASS: Your Honor, isn't it against the law to commit treason ?

THE COURT: If you go violating the law, you will go to jail. Now that will shut you off in the good work you say you are doing, you see.

DR. DOUGLASS: Don't you think it ,is against the !aw to commit treason ?

THE COURT: This is not committing treason. I know what treason is. This is not treason at all.

DR. DOUGLASS: I submit it is treason, Your Honor, when I let the Government use my money to support the enemies of my country. This is treason. I am being forced to break the law already. That is my whole point, Your Honor. I am being forced to break the law by paying this income tax which is being used against me and my family and my country. For instance, sir, the Sixteenth Amendment of the Constitution.--

THE COURT: Well, many people come around here and say that the Government is wrong and that they don't like to be drafted, and they don't like this and they don't like that. I can sympathize with them, Doctor. But we cannot maintain the solidarity necessary to keep this country alive and independent from Communism unless you and I and everybody else helps out. That is what we have to have.

DR. DOUGLASS: I have helped in every way I know how, Your Honor .

THE COURT: Huh? DR. DOUGLASS: I say, I have helped in every way I know how, and I will continue to do so.

THE COURT: Now, after you have made your protest, whether it is in this record or any place else -- you make all the protest you want. This is a free country and you have a right to do that. But you do not have a right to extend it to a violation of the law, you see.

DR. DOUGLASS: I understand that perfectly, Your Honor. As I say, I am being forced to break it

THE COURT: You are not a lawyer. I don't know whether you understand it or not.

DR. DOUGLASS: I understand, sir I am being forced to break the law. This is my point, sir. But, also, is it not true--

THE COURT: I think it would be better if, instead of listening to me, you would go get yourself a lawyer and let him tell you something that you pay for. Advice that comes to you free is usually not considered very much. I am not doing anything here at this time but telling you that after listening to you, your theory and your comment, that you have not shown a sufficient reason

28

for not paying your taxes -- for not producing your records. These people have a right to ask you that. You filed a thing like this -- I had it here a minute ago -- here it is -- and that is a red flag that sends them right to your office. You see that-

DR. DOUGLASS: I can respect that, Your Honor.

THE COURT: They are smart, you know that.

DR. DOUGLASS: May I quote Article 1, Section 8, of the United States Constitution?

THE COURT: What is that?

DR. DOUGLASS: The constitution specifically states that all taxes must be levied equally. And that has never been done from the very beginning. The whole l.R.S. system, the way it is set up, is unconstitutional. The tax is not equal in any sense of the word.

THE COURT: Where does it say that?

DR. DOUGLASS: Article 1, Section 8.

THE COURT: Yes, sir. Did you ever hear of the Sixteenth Amendment?

DR. DOUGLASS: Yes, sir. It does not say that the tax can be levied unequally. It says they may levy an income tax, but it does not say they can do it unequally.

THE COURT: Well, the reason we learned in history for the initial equality was a rule that prevented people from having income taxes, the very thing we are here for today. The Sixteenth Amendment says income tax is good, despite that previous ban on it, because the people of the United States have ratified a new amendment and income tax is what the people of the United States want. So we are away past that. Now, don't get --

DR. DOUGLASS: I beg your pardon, Your Honor. It does not say that the law can be applied unequally and that people can be taxed unequally. It does not say that.

THE COURT: The income tax law says that, doesn't it?

DR. DOUGLASS: No, sir.

THE COURT: Isn't it a graduated income tax?

DR. DOUGLASS: No, sir. The Sixteenth Amendment is very brief. The Sixteenth Amendment does not specify a graduated income tax. -- Do you have a copy of the Constitution here, sir? I can show you it does not state the tax can be levied unequally, and it is unconstitutional to do so, because Article 1, Section 8 of the Constitution says that all taxes will be applied equally.

THE COURT: Is there anything more you want to say, Doctor?

DR. DOUGLASS: Sir, may I continue?

THE COURT: Yes, go ahead.

DR. DOUGLASS: I am trying to save time sir, by going through some of this. Another reason I have refused to pay taxes

for 1965 is the fact that tax-exempt subversive organizations hiding behind a protective mantle of the Federal Government are riding herd on the American people. There are organizations that have been listed as subversive organizations that are still tax-exempt. This is another point I am trying to prove, the fact that money is being used against me, against my family, and against my country. I could name some of those for you, sir, but I will save time and I will go on. -- I will name one just for the record, if I may, sir.

THE COURT: Go ahead.

DR. DOUGLASS: There is an organization called the Metropolitan Music School, Incorporated. This is a Government-cited subversive

THE COURT: Wait a minute, Doctor. If you are going to go through all those things, I will agree with you that the Government makes mistakes, that there are probably people that are tax-exempt that ought not to be tax-exempt. There are probably people who ought to be tax- exempt who aren't. But those are mistakes. I don't want a whole list of them. I will agree such a thing might happen. But that doesn't go any further than that. Go ahead.

DR. DOUGLASS: I wanted to point out that this is a Government-cited front that still has tax-exemption. I think it is interesting to have something like that on the record. That is not the only one, there are many others.

Another example of the essential Communist control of the U.S. Government is the U.S. Department of Commerce.

THE COURT: Huh?.

DR. DOUGLASS: The U.S. Department of Commerce. While our forces in Viet Nam are fighting with defective arm munitions and worn out equipment -- and this has been in the Congressional Record -- the Commerce Department of the United States is encouraging American businessmen to ship billions of dollars of war materials to our enemies. To name a few for the record, we are sending to Russia and other Communist countries copper, polystyrene, wheat, entire steel mills, fertilizer plants, and various chemicals necessary for the making of war.

I would like to name for the record one. Secretary of State Dean Rusk. This is just one example of hundreds and hundreds of names that I can supply to you and to the Federal Government, if they want them, if they want to really fight Communism, of people who have long pro-Communist records, who have not been investigated and who are in top positions in our Government.

THE COURT: Well, now, Doctor, that won't do us any good in this session here today. If you want to send those to the Department of Justice or somebody --

THE COURT: Huh?

DR. DOUGLASS: I have, sir, and they have been ignored. Many people have sent these in and they do nothing about it.

THE COURT. Well it hasn't anything to do with collecting your personal income tax.

DR. DOUGLASS: Sir, don't you think it has when the Secretary of State is known to be a member of the Institute of Pacific Relations, a Government proven espionage ring? He was not only a member, he was an officer in that ring. And he is now Secretary of State, and he has never been investigated. Never.

THE COURT: As I say, if you are telling it right and it is the truth, it is a mistake. But two mistakes -- one mistake doesn't justify --

DR. DOUGLASS: Sir, I could list them for hours, but I don't want to take up your time. You are a very busy man.

THE COURT: Do you have anything else? Is it all summed up in the simple statement that you feel that you are in some way entitled to make a protest against the Communist matters that you have talked about by not paying taxes? Now, you are here today to be told that that is not a sufficient cause for failure to pay your taxes, and likewise not a sufficient cause for your failure to talk to these gentlemen who are trying to collect the taxes that you probably owe for 1965. So you are not going to get any release by making a protest in this fashion. You make a protest in the places where protests ought to be made. But you pay attention to your duty here to pay the taxes and to cooperate. If you have anything more, any other reasons, I want to get it on the record. But I don't want you to go into a very lengthy amplification of the same point.

DR. DOUGLASS: Well, my duty, sir, is it not true, is to do the best I can as an American citizen to protect and save my country? That is my first duty. My duty is not just to pay taxes, my duty is to be a good American .

THE COURT: That's right. There is more to it than paying taxes, sir. That's right.

DR. DOUGLASS: If there is a law that says you must cross the street here and then later on somebody digs a big ditch thirty feet across the, street there, and the sign still says you must cross the street there, then if you cross the street there, you are not only a fool, you are destroying everything that you want to do. The

31

law has been perverted, and some how or other someone has to protest against this law. I am not going to be forced into a thirty foot ditch and break my neck any longer. I have been doing it for too many years.

THE COURT: Well, Doctor, what kind of doctor are you-- an MD?

DR. DOUGLASS: Yes, sir. I am a general practitioner.

THE COURT: In Sarasota?

DR. DOUGLASS: Yes, sir.

THE COURT: I know you are an educated man, and I know from what you say that you are a person devoted to our country. And I know that there must be someone in the Government that you respect, isn't there?

DR. DOUGLASS: Oh, certainly, sir. Most of our Government employees are very good, able and dedicated people, including everyone in this room, I am sure. And I have nothing personal against this gentleman over here. (Indicating Mr. Davis)

THE COURT: And you must realize that you have no right to do this. And I am going to say to you that think that we have heard enough here to get the point of what your contention is, and I have said enough to tell you that it is not sufficient. Now, either you make arrangements to comply or you are going to feel the force of your Government. Now, that is up to you.

DR. DOUGLASS: I have been feeling the force of the Government for sometime, sir. As I said, they investigated me three out of four years for no reason other than--

THE COURT: I don't know whether they did right or not, but I am going to tell you that what is going to happen to you here is going to be right. That is my version of it. Now, you are going to have to do what the other 200,000,000 Americans are doing. You are not over in Viet Nam fighting anywhere. All you are asked to do is pay your taxes. That is all I am asked to do. And I am doing it, and you should do it. Now, what do you want to do here? These people are here for the purpose of making arrangements when they can see you at a convenient time for you and get this thing over with. And put your protest, as l say, in the place where you want to protest. You have a right to protest to anybody, and you can protest to them if you want to. -- Or to me, if you want to, which you have done. But you are going to have to comply with the requirements of taking care of this little business matter of your 1965 personal income taxes. That is what you are going to have to do. You can't avoid that, Doctor, and I am not going to let you. So you can take it in the right way or you can take it in the wrong way. But it is up to you.

Now, do you want to tell these people when they can see you or not?

DR. DOUGLASS: As I said earlier--

THE COURT: Don't get exasperated. Don't be thoughtless. Be sensible, and tell us what you want done.

DR. DOUGLASS: I have given this a lot of thought, Your Honor. I have been thinking about it for years. This is not an overnight decision on my part. I have given this a lot of thought. You said I am not in Viet Nam, sir, but I was eight years in the Military.

THE COURT: If you have never been told by anyone who has the right to tell you that you are wrong, why, you are being told now. What do you want to do? Do you want to defy the Government or do you want to comply?

DR. DOUGLASS: I am not trying to defy the Government, Your Honor, but as I told you earlier you will have to order me. If you order me, I will do it.

THE COURT: I am going to do that, Doctor.

DR. DOUGLASS: Because I have to obey the law, and I will do it.

THE COURT: There is no alternative to me sir. You understand my position?

DR. DOUGLASS: I certainly do sir. I understand your position.

THE COURT: If I were sitting in your position ,and you sat up here, sir, you would make the same ruling.

MR. FUERTH: Your Honor, may I interject this? I don't wish to change the order of procedure, but in view of the fact that this may receive some appellate review--I don't know what Dr. Douglass's intentions are -- would the Court indulge me and allow me to put on a little testimony and put the summons into the record?

THE COURT: Yes. We will make a record that will be complete while we are here, and let's have one hearing and one hearing only.

MR. FUERTH: Yes, I would like, if I may --

THE COURT: Do you want to ask the Doctor any questions?

MR. FUERTH: No. Really the only thing l would like to do, Your Honor, I would like to put Agent Davis on the stand and take his testimony here, and introduce the summons and the copy of the return, that you have in front of you, into evidence.

THE COURT: I don't think here is any dispute about it, but if you want the Agent to testify -- is this Mr. Davis here?

MR. FUERTH: Yes, sir, he is here.

THE COURT: Stand up, Mr. Davis, and take this oath.

THEREUPON:

> BLAKELY I. DAVIS
> a witness called on behalf of the
> Petitioners, having been first duly
> sworn, was examined and testified
> as follows:

DIRECT EXAMINATION

BY MR. FUERTH:

Q   Mr. Davis, will you give us your full name ?

A   Blakely I. Davis.

Q   And what is your address and your position in the Government?

A   I work out of the Sarasota office, which is on Orange Avenue in Sarasota. I am an Internal Revenue Agent

Q   With the Internal Revenue Service?

A   Yes, sir.

Q   And as such, what is your function?

A   It involves the investigation of assigned returns to determine the correct tax liability.

Q   Mr. Davis, I show you a return, copy of which has been given to the Court and to Dr. Douglass --

(Whereupon, Mr. Larry Sides, a friend and interventor on behalf of the Respondent, came forward and spoke with the Court in a low tone of voice not audible for the record.)

MR. SIDES: Could we have a recess, sir, so I wouldn't miss anything?

MR. FUERTH: Your Honor, is this gentleman a member of the Court, or--

MR. SIDES: No, no. I was just--

DR. DOUGLASS: He is a friend of mine. Just a friend.

THE COURT: He asked if he could have a conference with the Doctor outside the room, and I said he could. But I will not --I will insist the Doctor stay here while this man testifies. So that isn't going to work out.

MR. SIDES: I don't know the procedure. I am his friend.

THE COURT: Go ahead.

MR. FUERTH: Let the record reflect I have shown the witness an income tax return, copy of which has been submitted to Dr. Douglass and to the Court.

THE COURT: You understand we have the witness's affidavit already here in this file?

MR. FUERTH: Yes.

BY MR. FUERTH:

Q   Were you assigned that return to investigate?

A   Yes, sir.

Q   Approximately when?

A   Approximately June the 10th.

MR. FUERTH: At this time I would like to offer into evidence as Government's Exhibit No. 1 a copy of the Federal Income Tax Return.

THE COURT: Is this the same thing?

MR. FUERTH: The same as you have, Your Honor.

THE COURT: I will Mark it.

(Whereupon, the above-refereed document was marked by the Court as Government's Exhibit No. 1.)

BY MR. FUERTH:

Q   In connection with that investigation, did you have an opportunity to call upon Mr. Douglass?

A   Yes, sir, I did.

Q   When did you call upon him?

A   I called him by phone, my first contact with him.

Q   When was that?

A   This was on July the 7th of this year.

Q   I see. What did you ask him at that time?

A   Well, I told him that I had been assigned his 1965 tax return, and requested that he arrange an appointment when I could go over his books and records.

Q   Did he agree to the request?

A   No, he did not.

Q   Did you have a subsequent occasion to call upon him?

A   Yes, I did.

Q   When was that ?

A   I called on him at his office on August 30th of this year.

DR. DOUGLASS: May I interrupt, sir? Am I allowed to interject a question, or should I wait?

THE COURT: You will have an opportunity if you have any objections, when he finishes.

DR. DOUGLASS: I do have an objection.

THE COURT: What are you objecting to -

DR. DOUGLASS: I don't know if it is an objection or not. He came unannounced.

THE COURT: No, that is a question of fact. But it is not a question of whether --hat I mean by an objection would apply to the rule that he has to stay on the track, see.

DR. DOUGLASS: Yes, sir.

THE COURT: He is on it. Go ahead.

BY MR. FUERTH:

Q Mr. Davis, I show you here a copy of a Treasury Form 2039, copies of which I have submitted to Mr. Douglass and to the Court. On that particular occasion did you have that with you?

A Yes, sir, I did.

Q What did you do on that occasion with respect to that summons?

A I served a copy by delivering it to Dr. Douglass, personally.

Q On that occasion ?

A Yes, sir. On August 30th.

MR. FUERTH: At this time I would like to offer it into evidence.

THE COURT: Have you any objection to that, Doctor?

DR. DOUGLASS: No, sir.

THE COURT: All right, that will be Exhibit 2.

(Whereupon, the above-referenced document was marked by the Court as Government's Exhibit 2.)

BY MR. FUERTH:

Q Mr. Davis, this summons calls for Dr. Douglass's appearance at an office in the Federal Building at 111 South Orange Avenue, Sarasota, Florida, September 15th of 1966. Were you there at your office at that date?

A Yes, sir, I was.

Q And did Dr. Douglass appear?

A Yes, sir, he did.

Q Did he produce the records at that time?

A No, sir, he did not.

Q Can you tell us just briefly what transpired at that time?

A Well, Dr. Douglass visited the office with other individuals, who were unidentified. Mr. Foreman, my group supervisor, was in attendance, also. We went into a conference room. Dr. Douglass was asked by Mr. Foreman to identify those present. He declined to do so. He requested that he be shown some authority that he could not bring friends of his along. He also turned on a tape recorder which he had brought, and Mr. Foreman asked him to -- said that we could not allow the tape recorder on. He also wanted to be shown some provision of law where he could not record what went on.

At this particular point I injected myself into the conversation, asked Dr. Douglass if he had brought with him those records indicated on the summons. He said he had not. I told him at this point there was no further need to continue the meeting, since he had not complied with the summons. And the meeting was terminated some five minutes after it began.

Q Since that date have you had an opportunity to examine any of the records listed in the summons?

A No, sir.

Q Has Dr. Douglass contacted you and indicated that he was willing to al low you to examine those records in any way?

A No, sir.

Q Could you tell the Court just very briefly why you want to see the records that are involved in this summons?

A Well, the Court has before him, of course, the so-called return which has been filed. It shows neither income nor expenses. Naturally, the books and records maintained by a taxpayer summarize those transactions which enter into his tax liability. Without them, I felt that it was impossible in this particular case to try to reconstruct his income and expenses properly. And it appeared a normal request to make this computation by virtue of securing the books and records.

Q In other words, you need this information to determine the correct tax liability for Dr. Douglass for the year 1965; is that correct?

A Yes, sir.

MR. FUERTH :Thank you. I have no further questions.

THE COURT: Do you have any questions you would like to ask this gentleman, Doctor?

DR. DOUGLASS: I have some questions, sir, I would like to ask Mr. Fuerth is that the same?

THE COURT: No. It is the one that is a witness, Mr. Davis.

DR. DOUGLASS: Am I not allowed to ask him some questions? I would like to ask him some questions.

THE COURT: At a proper time. Right now it is Mr. Davis.

DR. DOUGLASS: I see.

THE COURT: Do you have any questions to ask him?

DR. DOUGLASS: No, sir, not really. I want to make a slight correction or addition. I would like to make an addition to what he said. I don't know what the proper term is.

THE COURT: You heard what he said?

DR. DOUGLASS: Yes, sir.

THE COURT: You have an opportunity of straightening him out, if you don't think it is right.

DR. DOUGLASS: Yes, sir. Only one minor --

THE COURT: You don't have any questions to ask him?

DR. DOUGLASS: One minor correction. No questions as such directed to him. Now, I would like to have -- I just want the record to state one thing. I have no questions -- no, sir, I have no questions to ask him.

THE COURT: All right. That is all right. Who else do you want to put on?

MR. FUERTH: I have no other witnesses.

THE COURT: You want to ask counsel a question?

DR. DOUGLASS: Yes, sir. First I would like to put something on the record, that is, that Mr. Davis --

THE COURT: Let's see what kind of a question it is, to see whether we ought to swear him or not. What did you want to know?

DR. DOUGLASS: Sir?

THE COURT: I will swear him if he is going to testify to anything.

DR. DOUGLASS: I would like to have him sworn, then. I would like to ask him some questions, if I may.

THE COURT: Are they evidentiary questions, or --

DR. DOUGLASS: It is only fair to have him sworn in if I am going to ask him questions. Is that unusual to swear them?

THE COURT. Just a minute. Have you anything further on your side of the case?

MR. FUERTH: I have nothing further. I rest my case, yes, Your Honor.

THE COURT: Do you want to put him on as a witness for you?

38

DR. DOUGLASS: I want to ask him some questions. It seems to me it is proper to have him under oath.

THE COURT: This is an adversary proceeding. The Government says they are through. Do you have anything?

DR. DOUGLASS: I would like to put him on as a witness for me.

THE COURT: Stand up and be sworn.

THEREUPON:

STEPHEN FUERTH
a witness called on behalf of the Respondent, having been first duly sworn, was examined and testified as follows:

MR. FUERTH: Your Honor, I would just like, for the record, to interject one objection, that I fail to see how my testimony can in any way be relevant.

THE COURT: I haven't the slightest idea. But we are going to make this as pertinent as possible. Let the Doctor ask -- first, I will ask you to put your name into the record.

THE WITNESS: My full name is Stephen G. Fuerth, F-u-e-r-t-h.

THE COURT: And what is your position?

THE WITNESS: I am a trial attorney with the Tax Division in the Department of Justice.

THE COURT: What do you want to ask him?

DR. DOUGLASS: Sir, do l get a copy of all the proceedings here? I do, don't I?

THE COURT: If you buy it. Only if you buy it. He is a reporter, you see.

DR. DOUGLASS: Yes. I would like to have a copy of the proceedings.

THE COURT: Do you want to ask him any questions?

DR. DOUGLASS: Yes, sir, I do.

THE COURT: Go ahead.

DIRECT EXAMINATION
BY DR. DOUGLASS:

Q   Mr. Fuerth, have you discussed this case with anyone in Washington?

MR. FUERTH: Your Honor, this is --

THE COURT: This is not right.

DR. DOUGLASS: Don't I have the right to know that; sir ?

THE COURT: Huh?

DR. DOUGLASS: Don't I have the right to know if he has discussed the case with anyone else in Washington?

THE COURT: No. You have a right to ask him anything relating to why you didn't produce these records when Mr. Davis came and asked for them.

DR. DOUGLASS: I don't have the right to ask him any other questions besides that? I don't have the right to ask him if he has discussed this case? I don't have the right to ask him that, what he has heard?

THE COURT: No, that is not fair. What do you want, Mr. Wilson?

MR. WILSON: Your Honor, as a matter of fact, under the Department of Justice Manual he can not testify to any of those facts without the consent of the Attorney General.

THE COURT: I thought, Doctor, you were going to question him something as to the reason why the agent, Mr. Davis, went to see you, that he was supposed to work out some arrangements with you, or something like that?

DR. DOUGLASS No. I merely wanted to know with whom he has discussed this case in Washington, and how much he knows about the case. That is all I wanted to know. It seemed like a fair question to me. I don't know what is the procedure.

THE COURT: I won't let you ask him that. Any other questions?

DR. DOUGLASS: No, sir, I have no other questions.

THE COURT: All through? Is there anything else you want to put on, Doctor? If there isn't --

DR. DOUGLASS: May I ask you a question, sir? I am not quite sure I understood your answer. I can not have a copy of this without paying for it, myself?

THE COURT: Not right now. You can't have anything until --we are going to complete this examination, and if you want a copy, you can buy it from him.

DR. DOUGLASS: May I have his name and address, sir?

THE COURT: Yes, he is the Official Court Reporter, Mr. Slemp here.

MR. WILSON: S-l-e-m-p.

THE COURT: Is there anything further to ask in this case, now? Let's move along.

DR. DOUGLASS: I don't believe I have any further questions, no, sir.

THE COURT: So now, then, I am going to make a ruling here that the order to show cause is properly served upon the defendant, Dr. Douglass, and that he has appeared and made a purported showing of cause, which is insufficient --

* * *

Whereupon Doctor Douglass agreed to allow the l.R.S. agent to see his books. The records were inspected and an estimated tax was levied. To this was added a "negligence penalty" of $128.85, a "delinquency penalty" of $644.23 and 6% interest amounting to $72.15. The victim was then presented with Form, 870 and asked to sign it. This form, in effect, waives a citizen's Constitutional rights and is a confession to crimes unnamed.

The doctor refused to sign the form and he continues to refuse to pay the tax and penalties.

MRS. WILLIAM HENRY SULLIVAN. Jr.
PRESIDENT GENERAL
NATIONAL SOCIETY DAUGHTERS OF THE AMERICAN REVOLUTION
ADMINISTRATION BUILDING, 1776 D STREET. N.W
WASHINGTON, D.C. 20006

August 14, 1967

The Honorable Stewart L. Udall
Secretary of the Interior

Dear Mr. Secretary:

No doubt you have been advised that Miss Joan Baez has advertised in the local newspapers stating that she is giving a "free concert" today, Monday, August 14th, at 8:30 p.m., on the Washington Monument grounds.

It is my understanding that the Washington Monument grounds are Federal property, supported by taxpayers' money. If this is the case, I respectfully request that Joan Baez be denied the privilege of using property supported by Federal taxes since it has been reported in the press that she refused to pay a portion of her own legal Federal taxes because of disagreement with Government policy concerning the Vietnam War. I question whether or not anyone is entitled to the privilege of using U.S. taxpayers' property for which he or she has not paid his fair share.

The reason for this request is the extreme concern of the more than 185,000 patriotic members of the National Society Daughters of the American Revolution and their families who pay several hundred million dollars per year in Federal taxes. As a result of traveling over 75,000 miles in the past twenty-four months, I have spoken with many thousands of citizens at the grass roots level of these United States. I am convinced that the mothers, fathers and relatives of our fighting men serving freedom's cause in Vietnam are greatly concerned about the expenditure of Federal tax money and would be even more concerned over the use of Federal property by anyone who refuses to pay his fair share of the Vietnam War tax burden.

Miss Baez' request to use Constitution Hall was denied because her public image and apparent objectives are clearly not in keeping with the Historic, Patriotic and Educational purposes for which the National Society Daughters of the American Revolution was chartered by the Congress of the United States.

Under the authority granted by Public Law 3553 of the 54th Congress of the United States of America, I respectfully request your immediate action to deny the use of Federal property to anyone who refuses to comply with the Federal laws of the United States Government.

Sincerely yours,

Mrs. William Henry Sullivan, Jr
President General, NSDAR

WILLIAM CAMPBELL DOUGLASS, M.D.
GENERAL PRACTICE
1812 HILLVIEW STREET
SARASOTA, FLORIDA

September 25, 1967

Mrs. William H. Sullivan, Jr.
President General
National Society Daughters of the American Revolution
Administration Building, 1776 D Street, N.W.
Washington, D. C. 20006

Dear Mrs. Sullivan:

Thank you for sending me the material I requested concerning your statements, in the name of the Daughters of the American Revolution, about Joan Baez's appearance on the Washington Monument grounds.

I agree with you most heartily that Communist collaborators like Baez should not be allowed to use government property. I would go a little farther: I think that anyone who preaches sedition should be arrested, given a prompt jury trial and, if convicted, shot. This would include, of course, the above mentioned J. Baez if so convicted.

However, I have some criticisms of your letter to the Secretary of the Interior Udall in which you urge that Joan Baez not be allowed to perform on Washington Monument grounds because she refused to pay her "fair share" of income tax. By disapproving of Baez's performance on this basis, you have fallen into a Communist dialectical trap. You are disapproving for the wrong reason. You have placed the D.A.R. into the unfortunate position of tacitly approving of the Marxist graduated income tax. I am sure this was not your intent but it was the ultimate result.

Joan Baez, with the help of the press and the unintended help given by your opposition, has achieved a two-prong Communist spywar objective: (1) The Communists are against the Johnson Administration's Viet Nam war and so it is patriotic to support this war in which our boys are "serving freedom's cause" and (2) the Communist-conceived graduated income tax is a "fair share" system, as American as apple pie and to pay it is to be patriotic and anti-Communist. Both of the above are, of course, false.

I will not dwell on the tragedy of the Viet Nam war and the danger it poses for American security because this letter is primarily about your unfortunate posture vis-a-vis the graduated income tax. I will only ask you one question concerning the war and your statement that our men are "serving freedom's cause": Who was the ultimate and only victor nation of World War I, World War II and the Korean War? Answer: Communist Russia. Russia and her collaborators around the world intend to keep these wars going until America is devoid of young men, energy, materials, money and morale.

Mrs. William H. Sullivan, Jr.
National Society Daughters of the American Revolution
Washington, D.C. 20006
September 25, 1967

Page 2

The greatest deception of all will be when the Communists can beguile the American people into defending, in the name of patriotism, the graduated income tax -- the sine qua non of Communism. It should be noted that Baez has not opposed the system of taxation. She has merely used this form of protest to dramatize her pretended opposition to the war in Viet Nam. How many Communists have you heard call for a repeal of the 16th Amendment, the amendment under which the graduated income tax was imposed? Would they oppose that which gives them their life's blood?

If great organizations like the D.A R. can be euchred into defending the graduated income tax, the hour is indeed late. By all means let us oppose the sullying of our great monuments by Communist traitors and revolutionists but let us oppose them because they are Communist traitors and not because they pretend to be in partial opposition to the tax system that has financed a large part of their world revolution.

This has been a harsh letter. I do not mean to impugn your sincerity or patriotism but I feel that the D.A. R. has made a serious tactical error in objecting to Joan Baez's performance on the basis of the income tax. The American people owe a great debt of gratitude to the D.A. R. which has stood up to the onslaught of Bolshevism in spite of smear from people who should know better and attacks from our home grown revolutionaries. I appreciate profoundly all that the D.A.R. has done and continues to do to preserve our Constitutional Republic and I hope that this frank letter will be received in the spirit of constructive criticism.

Yours for the Republic,

William Campbell Douglass, MD
WCD:r

MRS. WILLIAM HENRY SULLIVAN, Jr.
PRESIDENT GENERAL
NATIONAL SOCIETY DAUGHTERS OF THE AMERICAN REVOLUTION
ADMINISTRATION BUILDING, 1776 D STREET,N,W.
WASHINGTON 6, D.C.

October 13, 1967

Dear Dr. Douglass:

I appreciated receiving your letter of September 25th with your comments on the material sent out by the DAR at the time of the Joan Baez appearance on the Washington Monument grounds.

I am glad that you are in agreement with our not wanting this girl to sing in our Hall and I appreciate your frank letter sent in the spirit of constructive criticism. However you are incorrect in thinking that the DAR was tacitly approving " Marxist graduated income tax" by requesting Secretary UdaLL to deny Joan Baez the use of Federal property for her performance. My request to Secretary Udall was made on the basis of not allowing a lawbreaker to use property owned by the United States citizens who do obey the law.

So that you may have some further knowledge of the stand of the DAR on income tax, the "Income lax and Free Economy" resolution is enclosed.

Yours for victory and a free United States,

Mrs. William Henry Sullivan, Jr.
President General, NSDAR

Dr. William C. Douglass
1812 Hillview Street
Sarasota, Florida
i
Enclosure

Income Tax and Free Economy

Whereas, Unlimited money in the hands of government means unlimited power; and

Whereas, The federal Government has been given much of this power through passage of the 16th Amendment (the Federal Income Tax Law) wich has led to steadily increasing centralization and socialism, not with standing the fact that the several states already have the power to tax; and

Whereas. In the plan to destroy our system of government. the Communist Manifesto calls for heavily graduated income tax, abolishment of the right to inheritance through taxation, thereby inducing America to spend herself into National bankruptcy;

Resolved, The National Society, Daughters of the American Revolution urge the repeal of the 16th Amendment and support the proposed 23rd Amendment H.J. Resolution 355 which would remove the Federal government from the field of private business in competition with its own citizens and re-establish Constitutional protection of our free economy.

WILLIAM CAMPBELL DOUGLASS, M.D.
GENERAL PRACTICE
1812 HILLVIEW STREET
SARASOTA, FLORIDA

APR- 15, 1967

Mr. Henry Fowler
Secretary
U.S. Treasury
Washington 25, D.C.

Dear Mr. Secretary:

Supplementary to my letter of April 15,1966, which you did not answer, I would like to add the following information:

On July 7, 1966 a Mr. Blakely Davis of your Internal Revenue "Service " called me: "I have been assigned to check your 1965 records and return.-. I asked Mr. Davis if he had a search warrant and, after a long pause, he said that he did not. I then informed Mr. Davis that he could not see my records as I had had enough harassment from the Internal Revenue Service and l had no intention of revealing my records to him or to anyone else.

I informed Mr. Davis it is common knowledge that the IRS is using paid informers, various bugging devices, prostitutes, and other methods to harass American patriots and that I could in no way co-operate in this endeavor. It is obvious that if my records were obtained by IRS snoopers, they could harass my patients and therefore drive them from me and very quickly put me out of business. I certainly do not intend to cooperate in my own destruction. At this point Mr. Davis hung up saying that I would be hearing from him very shortly.

On the same day, July 7,1966, a Mr. Lee from the Internal Revenue Service called, advising me that I must pay a penalty of $122.40 plus interest because I did not file my 1964 income tax return in a manner satisfactory to him and his department. I informed Mr. Lee that I would pay nothing and if he wished to fine me he would have to take me before a court of law and, until such time that l was indicted for some criminal offense, to please leave me alone. He then threatened to attach my bank account and I told him to go ahead and do so if he could find it. He shouted: "I'll do just that" and hung up. This, as you know, Mr. Fowler, is a violation of Section 241, Title 18, United States Criminal Code which says: "If two or more persons conspire to injure, oppress, threaten or intimidate any citizen in the free exercise or enjoyment of any right or privilege secured to him by the Constitution or laws of the United States or because of his having so exercised the same,... (or they) shall be fined not more than $5,000 or imprisoned not more than 10 years, or both." At this time I have not heard further from Mr. L and he has not, to my knowledge, attempted to confiscate my proper When and if he does, I will swear out a warrant for his arrest hand him and take him to the nearest county jail. This is known as a citizen arrest.

On August 30, 1966, Mr. Blakely Davis, in the company of Mr. E. Foreman, arrived at my office unannounced and uninvited. They stat that they wanted to see my business records. In the previous fishing expeditions of 1963 and 1964 only one snooper was assigned to me. Why now takes two investigators to handle my small office was not explain

They first wanted to know who my two witnesses were and I refuse to identify them for reasons I am sure you can understand--retaliation not unknown in your Revenue Department. One of the two gentlemen Mr. Foreman, asked me why my companions were present. Although silly question, I answered him by stating that they were there to protect my interests.

When it became obvious to them that I was not going to reveal any personal records, Mr. Blakely Davis produced a "summons" which direct me to appear before him on the 15th of September, 1966, at 1:00 p.m. This so-called summons was illegal in that it did not come from any legitimate court but I complied with it and appeared at the Federal Building in Sarasota at 1:00 p.m. September 15, 1966 with five associates.

Mr. Blakely Davis and Mr. Foreman were again present and Mr. Fore man immediately asked me to identify my associates. I asked Mr. Foreman if it was required through the Internal Revenue Code for one to identify his colleagues and he said that he "had a right to know." I demand that he show me where in the laws of the United States it was necessary for me to identify my colleagues and he admitted that there was no such law. During this proceeding I had set up my tape recorder for the purpose of keeping proper records and Mr. Foreman objected violently this. He demanded that the tape recorder be turned off. I again asked Mr. Foreman to enlighten me as to where in the laws of the United State it stipulates that hearings are to be secret and tape recorders are not be allowed. We know, of course, that the Internal Revenue Service use them all the time. (See Senate Report No. 1053 March 4, 1966.) Mr. Foreman answered by stating that this could not be permitted. I again asked him to show me where the law stated that it could not be permitted and he had to admit there was no such law. I then informed Mr. Foreman that I was quite aware that there was no such law because I had checked it out in advance. Mr. Foreman then asked me if I was going to produce my records and I told him that, as I had reported to you in my letter of April 15,1966, which you did not answer, I could not for patriotic, moral and religious reasons comply with the illegally operated Internal Revenue Service and therefore that I could not produce my records. Mr. Foreman then said that there was no use in continuing the conference. Whereupon I packed up my tape recorder and left with my advisors.

I do not wish to be repetitious, Mr. Fowler, therefore I will not re peat any more than is necessary from my previous letter to you. But I would like to restate at this time that I am refusing to pay any further federal income tax because, after thorough investigation, I have come to the conclusion that the United States Government is now, for all practical purposes, controlled by the Communist conspiracy. I must therefore, for moral, religious and constitutional reasons refuse to pay any further federal income tax.

To substantiate this claim, from further research, since my last correspondence to you, I would like to append the following facts:

I insert there two broadcasts from Let Freedom Ring, the anti-communist telephone network, which clearly show the depths of depravity that have been reached in American affairs of state.

Their release of May 30,1967

If you are not sitting down, fellow American, we suggest that you do so before listening to this broadcast. For you are bound to be sickened by what we are going to tell you.

Last February, while America's sons were dying in Viet Nam fighting Russian trained and Russian equipped Communist troops, some of America's top generals and admirals were celebrating Russian Armed Forces Day in the Russian Embassy. What are our boys in Viet Nam going to think when they see their commanding officers drinking with Russian generals who are the brain behind the oriental fanatics who are trying to kill them in the swamps of Viet Nam?

What does it mean when our so-called leaders hobnob with the enemy? Does this explain why we are unable to win a

48

war against, a fifth rate rickshaw economy that is costing us two billion dollars and six hundred young lives a month? Isn't something tragically wrong when our troops have commanders who can fight the enemy one day and then booze it up with the enemy's top command the next day?

Representative John Rarick said recently " ... these generals and admirals have disgraced our flag and trampled under foot the faith and confidence of the people..."

Never before in history have so few paid such a high price for so many. From a poem by Josephine Beaty we quote:

> We prayed, "God, give us light
> That we may understand
> Why young men die in vain
> Far from their native land. "
>
> Then straightway came the answer,
> The old and proven truth --
> "When men betray and falter
> The price is paid by youth. "

Their release of June 6, 1967:

Last week we revealed that some of America's top military commanders were sipping cocktails with the Russian enemy while Americans were being maimed, tortured and killed in Viet Nam. In response to these atrocities, the State Department sends the enemy perfumed notes of protest which are quickly followed by machine tools, rocket engines and other materials of war.

"Peace at any price" is their motto. But what they really mean is that they and the majority of the voters are not being shot at. And as long as the Pentagon and State Department are not being bombed, there really isn't any war, is there? Peace at any price--even if it means killing off every American between the ages of 18 and 26.

One of Russia's alleged Cosmonauts, Yuri Gagarin, recently stated that Russian nationals have been fighting in Viet Nam all along. This information has been suppressed because the Johnson administration doesn't want American tax payers and parents to know that our government and the Russian government are in <u>collusion</u> in Viet Nam staging a phony but deadly war designed to weaken America to the point of helplessness. Former Secretary of Agriculture, Ezra Taft Benson, has said: "(there) appears to be a deliberate and determined effort to provide our enemies with the means to kill our sons."

America's fighting men are being betrayed in Viet Nam by a military leadership that seems unable to recognize the enemy and by civilian leadership that has a greater fear of death than love of country. The Richmond News Leader stated it well when they said: "Every Communist bullet that tears into American flesh in Viet Nam bears the brand of LBJ."

For documentation on this incredible story' see the Congressional Record, Feb. 27, 1967.

Lyndon Baines Johnson, President of the United States, has used tax monies previously paid by me and others to distribute 30,000 campaign pieces glorifying himself to the barber shops of the nation. The Department of Health, Education and Welfare has admitted sending these propaganda pieces out at taxpayers' expense. I cannot condone this and certainly cannot pay tax toward such a reprehensible project.

Lyndon Baines Johnson, President of the United States, has openly advocated treason as a national policy. By paying any further tax I would be supporting treason which is unconstitutional and I cannot be forced to commit treason against myself, my family and my country. The President of the Unite States, Lyndon Baines Johnson, has become so brazen that he can ask the American people to "sacrifice the blood of its children" in a hopeless war in Viet Nam (the way it is being fought) while at the same time asking for expansion of trade between the United States and the Soviet slave states which are supporting the Vietnamese war. This is clearly advocating treason as a national policy and, if I support it with my tax monies, I am guilty of defacto treason and defacto collaboration with my country's enemies. Our North Vietnamese Communist enemies are being protected right from the White House itself. By <u>direct order</u> of the President of the United States, strategic targets in North Viet Nam, including five airports near Hanoi, containing twin engine bombers, Soviet MiG fighters and electric power plants in the area, are protected from our Air Force.

The President of the United States has appointed Walt Whitman Rostow as Special Presidential Assistant. This puts at the elbow of the President a man who is such a serious security risk that when he was considered <u>for a high post in the</u> <u>United</u> <u>States Air Force</u> he was rejected. By paying taxes I would be contributing to this man's salary and therefore be committing defacto treason against my country.

President Johnson shows his strong bias in favor of our Communist enemies by allowing surplus farm products to be shipped to Egypt. Congressman Paul Fino reports that 40% of Egypt's rice crop has been sold or given to Communist China and Communist Cuba. Is it any wonder considering Mr. Johnson's record, that Gus Hall, head of the Communist Party U.S.A., came out openly for Lyndon Johnson's candidacy in 1964? While Americans languish in Russian and Chinese prisons and work on slave labor plantations behind the Iron Curtain, Lyndon Johnson announces: "The export-import bank is prepared to finance American exports for the Soviet-Italian Fiat auto plant. "So three-quarters of the machinery that Fiat installs for the Russians, who hold unknown numbers of Americans in slavery, will come from U. S. taxpayers. If Lyndon Johnson wants to finance vehicles for Russia, so that Russian officers can parade around in American made automobiles, let him take it out of his own pocket. (Reference: Henry J. Taylor, former Ambassador to Switzerland.)

The Soviet Union, through its own admission, is our principal enemy in Viet Nam and yet the President of the United States extends his hand to them. The President wants to send to the Russians vast quantities of grains which are now in very short supply in the United States. Total combat deaths as of September 24,1966 have reached 5,302 and yet the President helps the enemy kill more Americans. A mouthpiece for the Johnson administration, James Reston of the New York Times, now states that President Johnson is "prepared for a cease fire and a phased withdrawal of all combatants in Viet Nam." Even" "if this means a coalition with the Communists or even a Communist government." So American soldiers are dying in Viet Nam although the President of the United States himself admits that he would just as soon have a Communist government in the nation that we are supposedly defending against Communism. I cannot support a war with my tax money when that war is being fought to put the Communists in power.

As the President of the United States extends his hand to the enemy the Russians are conducting a huge arms airlift to North Viet Nam and Communist-controlled areas in Laos. This is not mere hearsay but was reported by the Joint Chiefs of Staff to the House Military Appropriations sub committee. The Joint Chiefs bluntly charge that if Russia is allowed to pour arms into North Viet Nam by air or sea, "thousands of Americans will die needlessly in South Viet Nam." General Wheeler said. "The Russian airlift is one of the largest they have ever operated. They are carrying every conceivable weapon." Lyndon Johnson, as official policy, is now helping our Russian enemies to augment their airlift to destroy the flower of American youth. This is simple treason and no other word will fit the case. I cannot under any circumstances contribute tax monies to support treason by the President or anyone else.

The President has further shown his willingness to collaborate with the enemy in using economic boycotts. The President obviously realized the effectiveness of economic boycott in that he has helped to use it in trying to destroy anti-Communist Rhodesia. While attacking Rhodesia with economic warfare, he extends the hand of commerce to our enemies in Asia. (See Congressional Record, Oct. 17, 1966.)

The Vice President, Hubert Horatio Humphrey, is now on official record as approving Communism in Russia, the United States and in all countries except in China. He said on October 5,1966, "Only in Asia does Communism still maintain its primitive and irrational militancy... we look ahead to the time when even Asian Communism may turn away from the path of force." Therefore we have the Vice President of the United States on record officially as approving of Communism in the United States, Russia, all of its slave satellites and eventually, all of the world. The Vice President of the United States has come out openly for a Negro revolution in the United States. He has even said that he himself could very easily lead this revolution. The Vice President is therefore inciting riot and revolution and I will not, under any circumstances, contribute to his treason by paying any portion of his salary.

The captive nations of the world, crying out for our assistance in over throwing their Russian slave masters, hold an annual affair called "Captive Nations Week." The Vice President of the United States, in typical Communist fashion, snubbed the Captive Nations dinner and went instead to an affair at the Communist Polish Embassy. When asked why he went to the dinner of this International Murder Incorporated instead of to the Captive Nations dinner Mr. Humphrey replied: "Because I wanted to be with these kind and friendly people." I cannot pay one iota of the salary of a man who is either an imbecile or a traitor.

Following the lead of the President and Vice President of the United States, various cabinet members have thrown all inhibitions to the winds and are now openly advocating treason, riots and anarchy. The U. S. Commissioner of Education, Mr. Harold Howe, II, for instance, is now openly advocating "black power" (black race supremacy). He has told Negro audiences not to "quiet down" but to continue their policy of hatred, murder and mayhem.

Secretary of the Interior, Stewart L. Udall, following the President's lead in treason, has announced that the Department has given its CONSERVATION SERVICE AWARD to Folk singer Woodie Guthrie. Mr. Guthrie has been identified as a Communist before the House Committee on Un-American Activities and therefore Mr. Udall is now giving my country's honors to an identified Communist agent. To further glorify this revolutionist, Mr. Udall has announced that a Bonneville Power Administration sub-station in the Pacific Northwest will be named after him.

Participating in this treason, and encouraged by the President of the United States and his Cabinet, are various American businessmen. These businessmen are supplying huge quantities of soy beans and tallow, both of which are necessary in the production of ammunition, to the Soviet bloc. If these American businessmen wish to sell the ingredients for ammunition to the Communist enemy then let them pay the taxes out of their sanguinary profits. Treason has become so rampant and open with the encouragement of the President and Vice President and members of their Cabinet, that wheat is being shipped directly from the port of New Orleans to Communist Cuba .

Also, following the President's lead in treason, is former Attorney General Nicholas Katzenbach who has used, as department policy, the covering up of the Communist influence in various racial revolutions around the nation. Although a Cleveland grand jury decided unequivocally that the riots in their city were fomented by trained Communist agitators, Mr. Katzenbach said they were caused by "disease and despair." The Attorney General of the United States is therefore using his position to cover up Communist revolution and I cannot under any circumstances contribute to this man's salary. The Johnson Administration has withheld from the American people the fact that Communist Negro revolutionaries are planning to burn Los Angeles to the ground and kill off all white males and children. White women are to be turned over to the revolutionary army. They have large quantities of anti-tank guns, grenades, machine guns and bazookas ready and the Negro fanatics to man them.

Instead of enforcing the sedition laws and the gun laws now on the books, which make it illegal to own such weapons of war, the Communist-controlled executive branch of our government is working furiously to beguile our congress into passing gun registration laws, the effect of which would be to disarm the American people by restricting the ownership of defensive guns and rifles.

It has come to my attention that the Fund for the Republic and the Center for the Study of Democratic Institutions are both being favored with tax exemption. This increases the tax load of all sincere and patriotic Americans. These tax-exempt groups openly advocate the abolition of private property. The Guggenheim Foundation is tax exempt and has subsidized such famous Communists as Langston Hughes and Louis Adamic. They have also given tax free money to Leroi Jones, a Negro revolutionist and Communist collaborator. They have also given tax free monies to Allen Ginsburg, pornographer and promoter of LSD among our youth. These foundations with tax immunity, are working assiduously for the decline and fall of our civilization.

Another tax-exempt organization that promotes Communism and revolution is the National Student's Association. This association is subsidized with about $600,000 from the tax-exempt Ford Foundation and the Rockefeller Foundation. Part of N.S.A. funds come from the Department of State and C.I.A. The Money then goes from N.S.A. to support the Student Non-Violent Coordinating Committee, S.N.I.C.C. Therefore the unwilling American taxpayer is being forced, through his tax money, to support S.N.I.C.C., the Negro equivalent of the K.K.K. Recently, Governor George Wallace of Alabama exposed an even more blatant and arrogant example of the United States government forcing the American tax-payer to finance revolution. He revealed that the United States government was financing the Black Panther Movement in Alabama, The Black Panther Movement is, of course, a Communist-controlled movement to murder white people. Any American who pays taxes under such conditions is supporting the destruction of Western civilization.

The International Committee of Conscience on Viet Nam, which appealed for the surrender of the United States to the Viet Cong, has tax deductibility. I demand at least equal rights with this committee, which demands the surrender of the United States to the enemy, and I therefore must insist on tax immunity so that my funds can be used to combat the conspiracy that the United States Government is financing

Professor Stephen Smale, a notorious Communist collaborator has received $91,500 in tax monies to travel to Russia. In Russia, Professor Smale denounced his country before a captive slave audience. The tax-payer financed National Science Foundation has made Professor Smale a glittering success and the average American wage earner and taxpayer would have to work 122 years to make the income to pay the taxes that made this traitor's trip possible. Any American who will put up with this by paying taxes does not deserve freedom.

An ex-convict by the name of Edward G. Partin was even forgiven $5,000 in back taxes because he acted as an informant for the Justice Department. He was under federal indictment for embezzlement and if convicted, faced 78 years in prison terms. Mr. Partin has not only failed to go to prison but has not even been made to pay back taxes. A law-abiding citizen would go to jail for much less

Why should not the Communists be happy with the United States Government since the end of World War II? From June 30, 1946 through June 30,1965, American taxpayers were forced, through an illegal tax process, to contribute a grand total of 193 million dollars of economic assistance to Communist Czechoslovakia, 573.6 million dollars in economic assistance to Communist Poland, 186.4 million dollars in economic assistance to the Soviet Union itself, and two billion, seven hundred sixty-one million, four hundred thousand dollars of economic and military assistance to Communist Yugoslavia. (See the Congressional Record July 20, 1966 page 15716.) How much in taxes does Polish slave boss Gromulka pay? How much in taxes does the butcher of Yugoslavia J. B. Tito pay? As a sovereign and free American citizen I demand at least equal rights with these Communist strong men. I will no longer allow you to force me to pay tribute, blackmail and bribery to various Communist mobsters around the world. By paying this tax I would not only be participating in defacto treason, I would be participating in defacto blackmail.

And speaking of blackmail, massive and brazen shakedowns have now become common with the federal government. The government threatened the Anheuser-Busch Company with an anti-trust suit but the company paid $10,000 in blackmail to Lyndon Johnson's campaign fund and the suit was promptly dropped.

When my case comes to trial before a jury of my peers, I will demand equal rights with certain Communist collaborators in the

United States government. I will demand to see the tax returns of the following: Harry Bridges; Gus Hall; William Mandel; Judge Constance; Baker Motley; Lyndon Baines Johnson; Hubert H. Humphrey; Adam Yarmolinski; Walt Whitman Rostow; Arthur Goldberg; Abbe Fortas; Dean Rusk; Lwellyn Thompson; Harold Howe, II; Orville Freeman; Nicholas Katzenbach; Walter Jenkins; Bobby Baker; James Harland Cleveland; Wilbur J. Cohen; Livingston Merchant; Dean Atcheson; Abba Swartz; Leonard Unger; Mrs. Esther Peterson Earl Warren; William O. Douglas; Ralph Bunche; Philip Jessup; Thurgood Marshal I; Robert C. Weaver; Foy Kohler; Adam Clayton Powell; former SEC Chairman, James M. Landis; the estate of Alben Barclay, former Vice President of the United States; the estates of Franklin D. Roosevelt and Mrs. Eleanor Roosevelt; the tax returns of Harry S. Truman, the return of the tax dodger, Dwight David Eisenhower; child killer Francis Medaille alias Michael J. Hanlon; Communist collaborator Ronald Ramsey, who takes broadcasts to Hanoi urging American soldiers to " lay down your arms"; Edward Clark, Ambassador to Australia; Anger Biddle Duke; Ambassador Walter Feldman; Treasury Secretary Henry Fowler; Assistant Attorney General Edwin L. Weisl, Jr.; Judge Anthony Celebreeze; Theodore Tannenwald; Howard F. Corcoran; Harold F. Lin Ja; Chairman of the Export-Import Bank, C. Douglas Dillon (alias Lapowsky); Anthony Akers, former Ambassador to Australia; Stokely Carmichael; former Indiana Governor Matthew Welsh, (Mr. Welsh receives $500 a week as a payoff from Lyndon Johnson. For this money he does nothing--his title is U.S. Representative of the American-Canadian Border Commission); Leonard Wolf; Donald Magnuson; Cory Knutson; Former Representative Merwin Coad; former Representative Catherine Granahan; former Representative Joseph Barr; former Representative James Quigley; Mr. Denver Hargis; Earl Hogan; Frank Kowalski; Frank E. Smith of the Tennessee Valley Authority; Mr. Fred Wampler of the Department of the Interior; Mr. Willard Wirtz, Secretary of Labor; General Hugh Hester; General Harry Vaughn; K. Penfield, Ambassador to Iceland and William Butterworth, Jr., Ambassador to Canada; (Both of these men are dangerous security risks, Butterworth has been named by a Chinese spy as a collaborator with Soviet intelligence.); Senators Gruening, Douglas, Saltonstall, Stephen Young of Ohio, McGee, Javits, and Kuchel of California; Edwin M. Martin, Ambassador to Argentina, and Daniel Frank Margolies, a Communist collaborator who is on special assignment from the State Department as Advisor to the President of the United States.

Many of the above are known security risks and Communist collaborators and it is clearly evident that it is official policy of the United States Government to maintain known and identified Communist enemy agents and Communist collaborators in key policy-making positions in the various departments of the United States Government. (See Defense Department Policy Paper entitled, "A Study of Historical Perceptions Concerning Allegations of Subversive Influence on the Far Eastern Policy of the United States Prior to 1949" and also Congressional Record of August 30,1966.)

In 1962 the United States government spent two and one-half billion dollars for economic and financial assistance to foreigners, two hundred and twenty-two million dollars for "foreign information and exchange, five billion dollars for farm income support and control of the American farmer, eight hundred and sixty-six million dollars to finance and control American aviation, five hundred seventy-five million dollars for subsidy and control of American business, six hundred seventy-five million dollars to buy houses for voters, five billion, one hundred million dollars for the illegal Department of Health, Education and Welfare and a billion and half for aid and control of American education. All of the above enumerated expenditures are totally unconstitutional and I refuse to contribute one penny to the support of unconstitutional federal so-called anti-poverty program, the objective of which is to totally demoralize the United States. As an example: one man hired recently at $8650 a year has been arrested as a pimp, forgerer and grand larcenist. Another man, hired at $4140 a year, is a sex criminal, as well as a larcenist. A Christine Bard has been hired as liaison officer for Project Headstart. Mrs. Bard is a prostitute who at one time ran a house of prostitution. These are only a few examples of the types of criminals, perverts and subversives that are being used in the Poverty Program to demoralize and destroy the United States of America. I will not under any circumstances and, no matter what the penalty, support these people in any fashion whatsoever.

The Department of Commerce is allowing the shipping of grinding machines to Russia (necessary for modern warfare), computer machines, electronic equipment of all types, oil, chemical plants, machine tools (which are the very heart of any industrial war making capacity), and such weapons of war as diesel engines, electronic computers and rocket engines. Instead of being paid a salary by American taxpayers, why hasn't the Secretary of Commerce been tried for treason? (See Congressional Record, Oct. 17, 1966.)

The Internal Security Sub-Committee of the United States Senate Judiciary Committee on July 30,1953 reported "The Soviet International Organization has carried on a successful and important penetration of the United States government and this penetration has not been fully exposed." What has been done to expose this conspiracy since 1953? Nothing. In fact, these very Communists and Communist collaborators are now persecuting American patriots through the Internal Revenue Service; the Justice Department; the Department of Agriculture; the Department of Health, Education and Welfare; the Department of the Interior, the Department of Labor and the Department of Urban Affairs. I will not be party to the harassment of American patriots through the paying of part of the salaries of these Communists and Communist collaborator.

The Internal Revenue Service unknown to most Americans, has become the federal mafia (along with the CIA). The Internal Revenue Service places "bugs" in public telephones, runs a snooping school at which a set of lock picks is given as a graduation present, employs wire taps against patriotic Americans, uses prostitutes and convicts for informant purposes and teaches its agents to lie under oath. I do not pro mote and defend criminals in my private life and I refuse to be forced to support government-promoted criminals.

You did not answer my last letter, Mr. Fowler. Will you answer this one?

Yours sincerely,

William Campbell Douglass, M. D.

WILLIAM CAMPBELL DOUGLASS, M.D.
GENERAL PRACTICE
1812 HILLVIEW STREET
SARASOTA, FLORIDA

APRIL 15, 1968

Mr. Henry Fowler
Secretary, United States Treasury
Washington, D. C.

Dear Mr. Secretary:

This dissertation on treason could go on indefinitely, but why continue a monologue that you refuse to challenge? If my case comes to trial, I intend to prove that the Internal Revenue Service is corrupt beyond belief. I have proof, for instance, that the IRS has railroaded decent citizens into the mental prison at Springfield, Missouri without benefit of trial. One of these victims has an affidavit by a qualified psychiatrist attesting to his sanity. A court appointed stooge psychiatrist had called this man, because he refused to knuckle under to the IRS, a paranoid schizophrenic. The victim has requested that I withhold his name because he is still quite frightened and on "probation." Complete documentation on this case is in my files.

The August, 1967, Reader's Digest only scratched the surface in its exposure of the Federal Tax Mafia. As a law-abiding citizen, I will not be forced to support a criminal gang that illegally and unconstitutionally seizes the property of our people in order to further oppress them.

On his last visit to my office, Mr. B. I. Davis of your tax collecting syndicate, came armed with a court order and examined my books. I was then fined, without benefit of trial, $845.23. Upon completing his "audit" Mr. Davis presented me with a summary of his findings and a Form 870 which he asked me to sign. What Form 870 says in essence is that I agree to the tax and the penalties imposed and that I confess to crimes unnamed.

You and your agent Davis are in violation of the Constitution of the United States by asking me to sign away my Constitutional Rights with your Form 870. Your action is not only a violation of the Fifth Amendment to the Constitution but also indirect violation of a recent Supreme Court ruling which states that no citizen can be forced to sign a statement that may later be used against him. This not only would apply to Form 870 but also to the income tax confession sheet, Form 1040. As you are aware Mr. Secretary, I have not paid the "tax due"; I have not paid the

U. S. TREASURY DEPARTMENT
INTERNAL REVENUE SERVICE

OFFICE OF THE DISTRICT DIRECTOR

111 South Orange Ave
Sarasota, Florida
January 19, 1967

IN REPLY REFER TO

I-8:BTD

William C. Douglass, M. D.
1812 Hillview
Sarasota, Florida

Re: Federal Income tax
     1965

Dear Dr. Douglass;

I am sorry that I missed you when I visited your office yesterday.

I have outlined below the results of the examination of your books and records for the year 1965.

Net profit from medical practice	$13,464.15
Interest income	45.03
Dividends (after exclusion)	-0-
Adjusted gross income	$13,509.18
Standard deduction	(500.00)
Personal exemptions	(1,800.00)
Taxable income	$11,209.18

Penalties:

Negligence 5% X $2,576.94   =   128.85
Delinquency 25% X $2,576.94   =   644.23
Addition for underpayment of estimated tax:
6% per annum computed on 70% of tax
liability for the period of underpayment   72.15

Total $ 3,422.17

I have enclosed Form 870 which reflects the tax, penalties and additions.
We have previously discussed the significance of execution of this form.
If there are any points you would like to discuss please phone me at 955-
6335.

After giving the matter you consideration, it would be appreciated if you
would contact me by January 25th to let me know whether you are in agreement with the proposals outlined herein, or, alternatively, that you intend to avail yourself of your rights to appeal.

Very truly yours,

B. I. Davis,
Internal Revenue Agent

61

FORM 870
(REV. FEB. 1965)

U. S. TREASURY DEPARTMENT · · · REVENUE SERVICE
WAIVER OF RESTRICTION ON ASSESSMENT AND
COLLECTION OF DEFICIENCY IN TAX AND
ACCEPTANCE OF OVERASSESSMENT

DATE RECEIVED BY
INTERNAL REVENUE
SERVICE

Pursuant to section 6213(d) of the Internal Revenue Code 1954 or corresponding provisions of prior internal revenue laws, the restrictions provided in section 6213(a) or corresponding provisions of prior internal revenue laws are hereby waived and consent is given to the assessment and collection of the following deficiencies, together with interest on the tax as provided by law; and the following overassessments are accepted as correct:

DEFICIENCIES

TAXABLE YEAR	TYPE OF TAX	AMOUNT OF TAX	PENALTY
1965	Income Tax	$2,576.94	$ 845.23

OVERASSESSMENTS

TAXABLE YEAR	TYPE OF TAX	AMOUNT OF TAX	PENALTY

NAME AND ADDRESS OF TAXPAYER(S) *(Number, street, city or town, State, ZIP code)*

William Douglass, M.D.
1812 Hillview Street
Sarasota, Florida

SIGNATURE		DATE	
SIGNATURE		DATE	
SIGNATURE	TITLE	DATE	

By

Corporate Seal

NOTE: The execution and filing of this waiver will expedite adjustment of the tax liability as indicated above. It is not, however, a final closing agreement under section 7121 of the Internal Revenue Code and does not preclude assertion of a further deficiency in the manner provided by law if it is later determined that additional tax is due; nor does it extend the statutory period of limitation for refund, assessment, or collection of the tax.

If the waiver is executed for a year for which a JOINT RETURN OF A HUSBAND AND WIFE was filed, it must be signed by both husband and wife unless one, acting under a power of attorney, signs as agent for the other.

If the taxpayer is a corporation, the waiver must be signed with the corporate name followed by the signature and title of the officer(s) duly authorized to sign. It is not necessary that the corporate seal be affixed. The space provided for the seal is for the convenience of corporations required by charter or by the laws of the jurisdiction in which they are incorporated to affix their corporate seals in the execution of instruments.

The waiver may be executed by the taxpayer's attorney or agent provided such action is specifically authorized by a power of attorney which, if not previously filed, must accompany the form.

If the waiver is executed by a person acting in a fiduciary capacity (such as executor, administrator, trustee, etc.), Form 56, "Notice of Fiduciary Relationship," should, unless previously filed, accompany this form

U.S. GOVERNMENT PRINTING OFFICE 1965 O -408-201

FORM **870** (REV. 2-65)

63

penalties and I have not signed away my rights as requested. Under Title 18, No. 2332, U.S. Criminal Code, it is considered <u>misprision of treason</u> to have knowledge of treason against the United States and not report it to the President, a judge of the United States, a judge of a particular state or a governor of a state. I have reported multiple acts of treason to you, a representative of the President, yearly for three years and have yet to receive a reply. Further conforming to Title 18, No. 2382, I will now send copies of these various letters, disclosing treasonous acts, to the Chief Justices of the various states and to the State Governors.

In order to continue to comply with the law as delineated under Title 18, No. 2382 and not be guilty of misprision of treason, I must report the following treasonous acts and circumstances to you, the Chief Justices of the State Supreme Courts and the State Governors:

The Justice Department says that they have no plans to prosecute Stokley Carmichael even though he openly declares his intention to destroy our country. By refusing to take action against Carmichael, Attorney General Ramsey Clark is <u>aiding and abetting rebellion</u>. I will not contribute to the salary of an Attorney General who violates Title 18, U.S. Criminal Code No. 2383 which states: "Whoever incites, sets on foot, assists, or engages in any rebellion or insurrection against the authority of the United States ... or <u>gives aid or comfort there to</u> , shall be fined not more than $10,000 or imprisoned not more than ten years, or both; and shall be incapable of holding any office under the United States."

President Johnson is also guilty of violating this Criminal Code The Communist revolutionary Stokley Carmichael got his start through Lyndon Johnson's Black Panther Movement in Alabama. Johnson's Office of Economic Opportunity financed this Mau Mau group and Carmichael quickly rose to fame therein.

Is not the House of Representatives guilty of misprision of treason when they fail to impeach Lyndon B. Johnson and literally hundreds under him for their violation of Title 18, U.S. Code No. 2381? <u>You do not have to be in an officially declared war, Mr. Secretary, to be prosecuted for treason</u> and receive the death penalty if convicted. Title 18, U.S. Code No. 2381 is clear and unequivocal: "Whoever owing allegiance to the United States, levies war against them or <u>adheres to their enemies</u> <u>giving them aid or comfort within the United States or</u> <u>elsewhere</u>, is guilty of treason and shall suffer death, or shall be imprisoned not less than five years and shall be fined not less than $10,000; and shall be incapable of holding any office under the United States."

President Lyndon Johnson's disloyalty to this country has become so obvious that it would be impossible to refute it. I will clearly delineate some examples of his treason and why I therefore refuse to pay one iota of his salary. The following is only a brief resume of his recent treasonous acts and statements:

President Lyndon Johnson: "We shall continue to build bridges across the gulf which has divided us."

Joseph Stalin." ...we shall build a bridge between East and West. "

Lyndon Johnson Oct. 7,1966: The President bragged that "we have just concluded an air agreement with the Soviet Union... (we have agreed to open direct air flights with the Soviet Union...")

Moscow New Times Nov. 16, 1966: "I am modest enough to say that I realized the importance of this victory at once. (the resumption of East-West flights) I knew that anti-Communism had received a crushing blow. " *

Lyndon Johnson: "Where possible, we shall work with the East to build a lasting peace. We do not intend to let our differences in Viet Nam... ever prevent us from exploring all opportunities."

Major Alexandrescu, Commandant of the prison in Communist Rumania: (Speaking to American prisoners) "You... expect the Americans to come and release you. Now I will give you the news. The Americans come, but not to release you. They come to help us... The Americans, if you beg them, they give you nothing. If you insult them, if you mock them, they give you money. "

The President "We have... determined that the Export-Import Bank can allow commercial credits to (Communist) Poland,"

A German newspaper reporting Oct. 1, 1966: "Weapons of the Polish Armed Forces are being shipped from the Stettin Harbor in ever increasing quantities to North Vietnamese Harbors..."

* Written by a Communist in Russia, publication.

65

The President: "We have... determined that the Export-Import Bank can allow commercial credits to (Communist) Bulgaria. "

The Premier of Communist Bulgaria Dec. 1, 1966: "The Bulgarian Government has extended and will continue to extend moral, political support and material aid to the Vietnamese people to bolster their economic and defense capability."

The President: "We have... determined that the Export-Import Bank can allow commercial credits to (Communist) Hungary."

Mr. Janos Kadar, the slave boss of Hungary, Dec. 3, 1966: "We are fighting against U.S. aggression in Viet Nam and will go on helping our Vietnamese brothers until their cause is crowned with an ultimate victory."

The President: "We have... determined that the Export-Import Bank can allow commercial credits to (Communist) Czechoslovakia. "

Communist Radio Prague, Czechoslovakia: "The entire socialist world has joined forces to provide Viet Nam with all conceivable assistance--economic, financial and technical as well as political, including the Soviet offer to allow volunteers from Czechoslovakia, the Soviet Union and other Socialist countries to go to Viet Nam."

The President (referring to Communist trade): "This is good business. "

See above and recent Viet Nam casualty lists.

The President: "We have... determined that the Export-Import Bank can allow commercial credits to (Communist) Yugoslavia."

Vladimir Popovic, top Yugoslavian official, says that the United States is guilty of "aggression" in Viet Nam and he called for Communist victory throughout the world.

The President: Oct. 7, 1966 "We have just signed a new United States-Soviet Cultural agreement. I am asking for early

S.P. Rashidov, a top Communist official: "The Soviet Union is supplying the fraternal people of Viet Nam with the most

Congressional action on the United States-Soviet consular agreement. The Export-Import Bank is prepared to finance exports for the Soviet Italian Fiat auto plant..."

modern weapons for meeting U.S. aggression. We are doing everything in order that the deliveries of Soviet military equipment-aircraft, rockets, artillery, ammunition and soon-will get into the hands of the Vietnamese freedom fighters as rapidly as possible. We Soviet people are happy that the military equipment which the workers of the land of the Soviets are producing at their enterprises with such great enthusiasm also helps the cause of victory of our (North) Vietnamese brothers over the aggressor... "

Congressman Poole of the House Committee on Un-American Activities said recently: "This Committee recognizes the right of every citizen to disagree with the foreign policies of the United States Government. It does not believe, however, that the Constitution gives any citizen, in the time of actual undeclared war; the right to assist the enemies of this country... by sending aid to them in any form... aiding an enemy of your country in time of war has always been regarded as treason..." Mr. Poole was not referring to the President when he made this statement-but he should have been. The next time you sign the President's pay check, Mr. Secretary, you might remember the above and you might also remember that the check includes no income tax monies of mine.

Since my first letter to you, Mr. Secretary, there has been an important change in White House personnel. Mr. Walt Whitman Rostow has been named as Special Assistant to the President for National Security Affairs. In my first letter to you I said of Mr. Rostow: "This man is such a serious security risk that when he was considered for a high post in the U. S. Air Force he was rejected." In spite of the fact that Rostow has been denied security clearance twice because of his pro-Communist background, the President himself has cleared Rostow to work as his aide. This has an interesting parallel in recent history: Walt Whitman Rostow is now playing Alner Hiss to Lyndon Johnson's Roosevelt. I can not, without participating in an act of treason, contribute to the salary of "Presidential Advisor" Rostow or his White House stooge.

In order to continue to comply with the law as delineated under Title 18, No. 2382 and not be guilty of misprision of treason, I must report the following treasonous acts and circumstances to you, the Chief Justices of the State Supreme Courts and the State Governors:

Did you know, Mr. Secretary, that ships owned by the United States Government itself, are being used to ship war supplies to North Viet Nam? (See reports of Senators Mundt and Hanson.) Senator Hanson expressed the sentiments of this ex-taxpayer quite well when he said: "The mothers, wives, and children of our men dead in Viet Nam can take little comfort that the weapon which killed their loved one reached Viet Nam in an American ship."

Most American taxpayers--to say nothing of the boys who are dying in Viet Nam--are not aware that Lyndon Johnson has the Army Corps of Engineers working with Russians, side by side, building an all weather highway from Russia to North Viet Nam so that Russia's weapons can get to North Viet Nam quicker and cheaper to kill more Americans. It will be quite a spectacle to see American taxpayer-financed Fiat trucks carrying American taxpayer-financed aircraft parts, radar, rocket engines and other war materials to North Viet Nam on a road that was built by American taxpayers for use by the Russian enemy. In case this little item has escaped your attention, the contract number for this Treason Road is Corps of Engineers Contract No. DA-92-144-Eng-73. Lyndon Johnson recently stated that he wants a ten percent surtax for the war effort. The only question is: For which side?

It should be noted here, for the benefit of those who still pay taxes that they are being forced, through the paying of taxes, to finance the destruction of the American educational system. The National Education Association, which is tearing our educational system to shreds and injecting the teaching of a Bolshevik philosophy into the public schools, is being financed in part by none other than the Communist-dominated Central Intelligence Agency. This, of course, seems incredible but I challenge the National Education Association to deny it.

Why should I pay taxes to support a Justice Department that will not prosecute traitors and even if they were prosecuted and convicted, would not put them in jail? The Justice Department has announced that it is dropping its espionage charges against Judith "The Mattress" Copeland. This traitor has been twice convicted but has never served a day in jail. Copeland was

68

found guilty of having stolen secret Government papers and for conspiracy to commit espionage, One intelligence report revealed that as a result of activities traceable to Copeland, over 500 dedicated anti-Communist patriots, behind the Iron Curtain were tortured and put to death. The Department of Justice showed criminal negligence in permitting Copeland to stay on her job. It showed criminal negligence in the preparation of the cases against her which allowed her to eventually go free. One can only assume that a conspiracy exists within the Department of Justice to protect traitors such as Judith "The Mattress" Copeland.

While setting free communist espionage agents, even though they have been convicted, the Government persecutes small people who have no important contacts but have the unfortunate attribute of loving their country. A Mr. Frank Marano was recently arrested and interrogated for selling bumper stickers that suggested if you don't like this country you should get out. He was told that he could not solicit for Americanism for then the authorities would have to give the same rights to subversives! But, as you and I both know, subversives already have these rights. The Mayor of New York City, for instance, is willing to give a permit to any left wing or Communist group any time they want to hold public meetings in the city for the purpose of burning the American flag and denouncing everything American. As Representative Paul Fino has pointed out in regard to this case; "There is something wrong when a disabled veteran is arrested in a public park for patriotism while Stokley Carmichael, Rap Brown and others incite rebellion throughout the land." I would like to add to this there is something drastically wrong when communist espionage agents who have done immeasurable harm to their country are protected by the Department of Justice and yet a veteran is persecuted for suggesting that anti-Americans should get out of our country if they don't like it. (Ref: Congressional Record Aug. 17, 1967, Page Hl0751.)

Even more astonishing than the above is the recent order sent to all Naval District Commanders in the U.S. instructing them not to allow units to participate in parades demonstrating support to four troops in Viet Nam! (Ref Houston Tribune, 8/24/67)

Not only the President and the Justice Department but even the Pentagon is harboring criminals and communist spies. Right in the heart of the American military establishment communist and communist agents are tolerated and actually protected. Robert Arthur Neimann although he has a number of Communist

affiliations and has proven beyond a doubt his loyalty to a foreign ideology, has been cleared for secret work by the Pentagon.
Security agents have been stunned by the action of the Pentagon
on this case but they should not be. This is only one of the many
examples of how the United States Government is vigorously
protecting and defending communist agents and communist collaborators.

Internal security has become a thing of the past in the
United States. The present administration and previous adminis-
trations have thrown the doors wide open to conspirators and
have actually welcomed them and protected them. Consider the
following breaches of security:

A foreign service officer who was found out to be a forgerer
has been given an important assignment right in the White
House. A security officer in Greece was revealed to have protected violators of security regulations but was appointed Deputy
Chief of Division of Security Evaluations at the State Department!
The Mutual Security Agency classified one government employee
as a definite security risk and said he had a "rotten file." But he
has been appointed to the State Department with a full security
clearance. One foreign service officer has admitted that he furnished 18 documents, some of them classified as secret, to the
publisher of the pro-communist magazine Amerasia. This officer
was permitted to retire honorably and is now living off the
American taxpayers. An admitted homosexual, considered unfit
to serve abroad because of his perversion, was not only sent over-
seas but was given a critical post behind the Iron Curtain. One
foreign service officer was known to be a member of the Young
Communist League and the Communist Party but is still em-
ployed by the United States State Department. Although a
known homosexual, who supervised Marine Guard personnel
and was protector of all safe combinations at the American Embassy in one foreign country, he was so negligent that classified
material got into the hands of the enemy. He was not disciplined
and is still being supported by the United States taxpayer in the
Department of State. (Ref: Mr. Clark Mollenhoff, the Des Moines
Register)

One of the most fraudulent uses of taxpayers money, and
one to which I will not contribute, is the so-called War on Poverty.
The United States Employment Service admits that there are over
four million jobs that remain unfilled in this country and yet the
American taxpayer is forced to pay degenerates to loaf, riot and
reproduce.

The communists themselves openly admit in their publications that the War on Poverty is their major weapon in bringing the Proletarian Revolution to America. Writing in an international Communist publication, Henry Winston, a well known Communist revolutionary, said: "Today, the Economic Opportunity Act (the official title of the War on Poverty)... has already become the basis for organizing struggles in the slums and ghetto communities and it offers the point of departure for helping to rally the rank and file millions into a powerful mass movement... "Thus, the Communists Freely admit that the American tax-payer is bankrolling the Communization of America. A $247,407.00 War on Poverty grant has been given to 100 union officials so that these labor agitators can use, taxpayers money to harness this proletarian communist revolution in America. As I said in my first letter, Mr. Secretary, contributing to this sort of madness is suicide and I will not be forced to commit suicide. War on Poverty funds are being used to promote and support bastardy, prostitution, sex perversion and bigamy. In New York City alone 436,000 women are receiving Aid to Dependent Children funds. 75 per cent of these children are illegitimate. These bastard children, a large percentage of which are Negroes and Puerto Ricans, will grow up and go on the relief rolls and reproduce themselves ten times over. Each of these ten turn will multiply them selves this <u>cultural and racial subversion</u> of America. This ten times over. The American taxpayers are being forced to finance process will continue, if it is not stopped, until the country falls from the weight of incompetent degenerate bastard children and their slovenly parents, in-laws, aunts and uncles, half brothers and half sisters, incestual husbands and wives etc. These creatures will tear at the flesh of the few remaining productive, intelligent, law-abiding citizens until the United States Government collapses under a morass of filth, disease, bloodshed, rapine and anarchy. <u>I maintain that this cultural and racial subversion is just as deliberate as the subversion of our national defense and the attack on America's Police</u>. It will, if the American people continue to finance it, lead to the fall of our country to Communism without a shot being fired.

Adding to this headlong rush into degeneracy and anarchy is the Civil Service Commission. Beatniks, homosexuals and alcoholics are to have preference for good positions over normal people! Directive No. 300-6 of the Civil Service Commission states "(Deviates) are now to be given every opportunity for advancement." The directive goes on to state that the privileged perverts and rummies <u>do not even have to</u> have a Civil Service Commis-</u><u>sion rating</u>(such as is require of those unfortunate people who happen to be afflicted with normal sexual habits, good manners and a sense of responsibility.) I will go to jail, Mr. Secretary before I will support this <u>deliberate</u> <u>corruption</u> of my government.

The Bolshevist character of the so-called War on Poverty is only lightly veiled. Representative Gubser of California found that one anti poverty headquarters, financed by the American taxpayer to the tune of $246,836.00, actually features on its bulletin board a picture of Red Chinese Defense Minister Lin Piao.

The evidence that the so-called War on Poverty is really a Communist revolutionary bettering ram is almost endless. One of the farmer's coops in a southern state recently received $700,000.00 from the American taxpayer. Among the members of this co-op are John Zippert a Communist-fronter, Shirley Mesher also a Communist-fronter and a supporter of the Black Panther Movement and other such revolutionary groups. One Communist in a Louisiana anti-poverty program was found to be getting $4200.00 in tax money with which to conduct his subversive activities. Unknown to the American taxpayers, they have contributed $28,000.00 to the Communist Ann Braden and other such Communist revolutionists through the West End Community Council of Louisville, Kentucky. The Blackman's Volunteer Liberation Army, the shock troops for the planned massacre of American whites, is partially financed by the War on Poverty. Sargent Shriver, head of the anti-poverty program, is clearly in violation of Title 18, United States Criminal Code No. 2383 concerning aiding and assisting rebellion or insurrection against the authority of the United States. Why has he not been arrested?

Aid to the enemy has reached even more shocking proportions since my last letter to you, Mr. Secretary, and again, in order to comply with Title 18, U.S. Code No. 2382-1 must report this disloyalty to our men in Viet Nam. The Dallas Times Herald of February 15, 1967 reported that there are now 100,000 <u>Chinese</u> troops in Viet Nam killing Americans. Yet, the Johnson Administration is allowing drugs to be shipped to Red China. Fearing the wrath of the American people, the Johnson Administration and specifically the Department of Commerce, made no announcement of this aid to the enemy.

While Americans are being <u>beheaded</u> in Viet Nam, your Treasury Department, Mr. Fowler, has granted permission to Yale students to send medical supplies to North Viet Nam. If you are aware of this permit Mr. Secretary, you are in my opinion, guilty of murder.

Although our boys in Viet Nam will see drugs from American Companies on the bodies of the enemy and they are now finding medical supplies and plasma marked "Berkley, Calif." or "Yale University, New Haven, Conn.," perhaps they feel lucky compared to the <u>800 Americans including women and children</u> who are rotting in Castro's prisons, ignored and forgotten by Bridge Builder Lyndon Johnson and his coterie of cowards, perverts and criminals.

The Administration has dropped practically all pretense at loyalty to American troops in Viet Nam. Being shipped directly to the Soviet Union are propeller blades, gun wadding, parachute cloth and shell stock. The American taxpayer this year will be forced to partially finance Communist Dictator Nasser's Palestine Liberation Army. <u>The principal function of this group is to recruit Arabs to fight for the Viet Cong</u>. While the American taxpayer is financing this Viet Cong recruiting agency, Radio Cairo, <u>operating over equipment furnished by the</u> United States, urges race war in the United States.

The American people have been deluded into thinking that the rich pay excessively heavy taxes. This is not true. The low income, middle income and moderately high income professionals pay almost all of the tax. The very wealthy, many of whom cooperate with the communist conspiracy, have learned to hide behind foundations of which there are now about 100,000, according to Representative Wright Patman. Many of these foundations are sub rosa conduits for CIA money that is channeled into communist and pro-communist revolutionary groups. The Ford Foundation, for instance, has granted $175,000 to CORE-- a Negro racial fanatic group. The money will be used, according to CORE head McKissick, to bring revolution to the city of Cleveland.

Unknown to the long-suffering American taxpayer is the fact that we are supporting both sides in the Arab-Israeli War. The American taxpayer is financing the training of Arab pilots at Randolph and Lackland Air Force Bases, Wichita Falls, Amarillo, Texas and in Colorado and Illinois. These Arab communist pilots are being shown military equipment that is considered to be too secret for the United States public to be informed of it. These soldiers then return to their homeland and share their newly found top secrets with their Soviet advisors-- compliments of the biggest sucker in the history of the world: The American taxpayer. The taxpaying milk cows, known as United States citizens, are actually being forced to provide, through their taxes, F-104 jet Fighters and M-48 tanks for pro-Communist Jordan. Soviet Air Force technicians are using this equipment in Jordan--and probably even in Russia itself.

Although the Government of Syria has denounced the United States as an aggressor in Viet Nam, has welcomed a Viet Cong delegation to Damascus and has collaborated with Communist China to provide weapons in the Arab-Israeli War, the United States State Department is training Syrian officers. If you wish to support the Arabs or the Israelis in this carefully engineered war, Mr. Secretary, I cannot stop you but don't count on using any of my money.

America's number one product is <u>war</u>. <u>Not</u> war against communism or war to protect America from tyranny but war merely for the sake of being at war. War for the sake of supporting a failing socialized economy; war to bamboozle the American people into accepting a tyrant in the White House and an eventual communist dictatorship. No patriotic American would refuse to finance or fight in a war to protect his country. But no American should pay taxes merely for the sake of keeping politicians in office. No American should die in a foreign war, Financed by the American taxpayers on both sides, that he is not allowed to win while the Chief Justice of the United States Supreme Court celebrates the Fourth of July in the camp of the enemy--at taxpayers expense. While Supreme Court Justice Warren was visiting his Communist friends in Poland, a Polish delegation returning from North Viet Nam said: "We are glad that Polish guns are bringing some concrete results..." No American should finance the war in Viet Nam or allow his son to die there when our <u>own State Department</u> <u>apologizes</u> to the Kremlin because American planes damaged a Soviet ship bringing <u>munitions</u> to our Army's enemies.

I have recently discovered in my reading, Mr. Secretary, that you also have an interesting background. Are <u>you</u> a Communist <u>too</u>? If you are, then I have misjudged you--you are not naive after all. Being a Communist collaborator would explain why you furthered the career of <u>identified Communist</u> Charles Flato. Being a Communist collaborator would explain why you furthered the career of <u>identified Communist</u> Harry Magdoff. Another identified Communist, Irving Kaplan, was so fearful of being as-

74

sociated with you that, on being asked, before a Congressional Committee, if he knew you, he <u>refused to</u> <u>answer on the grounds that it would tend to incriminate him</u>.

Being a deliberate collaborator with the Communist conspiracy would explain why you joined, two years after it had been cited by a Government committee as a front for Communist Russia, the Southern Conference for Human Welfare. Being a willing tool of the Communists would explain why you are sabotaging the dollar by attempting to remove all gold backing from it and why you have let ten billion dollars of gold slip out of our vaults and into the hands of Communist satraps like Charles De Gaulle.

In conclusion, I would like to quote to you from Cicero who very brilliantly described all of you who are knocking down the pillars of Western civilization. Cicero said: "A nation can survive its fools, and even the ambitious. But it cannot survive treason from within...for the traitor appears no traitor; he speaks in the accents familiar to his victims, and he wears their face and their garments, and he appeals to the baseness that lies deep within the hearts of all men. He rots the soul of a nation; he works secretly and unknown in the night to undermine the pillars of a city; he infects the body politic so that it can no longer resist. A murderer is less to be feared. The traitor is the carrier of the plague."

Sincerely yours,

William Campbell Douglass, MD

WCD:n

EPILOGUE

These letters are in no way meant to be a comprehensive coverage of the appalling situation that exists in this country nor is the listing of individuals more than a sampling of thieves, traitors and turncoats. The Letters are merely "a taste of treason" and it is hoped that they will lead the reader into further research and then action -- while there is still time. The following sources are recommended for further reading:

American Opinion Magazine, Belmont, Massachusetts 02178

American Way Features, Box 12533, Nashville, Tennessee 37212

The Network of Patriotic Letter Writers, Box 2003-D, Pasadena, California

Dan Smoot Report, P.O. Box 9538, Lakewood Station, Dallas, Texas 75214

Independent American Publications, Box 4223, New Orleans, Louisiana 70118

Capell Publications, Box 3, Zarephath, New Jersey 08890

Christian Crusade, P.O. Box 977, Tulsa, Oklahoma 74102
Let Freedom Ring (National Anti-Communist Telephone Network), Box 1775, Sarasota, Florida 33578

The Review of the News, Belmont, Massachusetts 02178

About Doctor William Campbell Douglass II

Dr. Douglass reveals medical truths, and deceptions, often at risk of being labeled heretical. He is consumed by a passion for living a long healthy life, and wants his readers to share that passion. Their health and well-being comes first. He is anti-dogmatic, and unwavering in his dedication to improve the quality of life of his readers. He has been called "the conscience of modern medicine," a "medical maverick," and has been voted "Doctor of the Year" by the National Health Federation. His medical experiences are far reaching-from battling malaria in Central America - to fighting deadly epidemics at his own health clinic in Africa - to flying with U.S. Navy crews as a flight surgeon - to working for 10 years in emergency medicine here in the States. These learning experiences, not to mention his keen storytelling ability and wit, make Dr. Douglass' newsletters (Daily Dose and Real Health) and books uniquely interesting and fun to read. He shares his no-frills, no-bull approach to health care, often amazing his readers by telling them to ignore many widely-hyped good-health practices (like staying away from red meat, avoiding coffee, and eating like a bird), and start living again by eating REAL food, taking some inexpensive supplements, and doing the pleasurable things that make life livable. Readers get all this, plus they learn how to burn fat, prevent cancer, boost libido, and so much more. And, Dr. Douglass is not afraid to challenge the latest studies that come out, and share the real story with his readers. Dr. William C. Douglass has led a colorful, rebellious, and crusading life. Not many physicians would dare put their professional reputations on the line as many times as this courageous healer has. A vocal opponent of "business-as-usual" medicine, Dr. Douglass has championed patients' rights and physician commitment to wellness throughout his career. This dedicated physician has repeatedly gone far beyond the call of duty in his work to spread the truth about alternative therapies. For a full year, he endured economic and physical hardship to work with physicians at the Pasteur Institute in St. Petersburg, Russia, where advanced research on photoluminescence was being conducted. Dr. Douglass comes from a distinguished family of physicians. He is the fourth generation Douglass to practice medicine, and his son is also a physician. Dr. Douglass graduated from the University of Rochester, the Miami School of Medicine, and the Naval School of Aviation and Space Medicine.

Dr. William Campbell Douglass'
Real Health:

Had Enough?

Enough turkey burgers and sprouts?

Enough forcing gallons of water down your throat?

Enough exercising until you can barely breathe?

Before you give up everything just because "everyone" says it's healthy...

Learn the facts from Dr. William Campbell Douglass, medicine's most acclaimed myth-buster. In every issue of Dr. Douglass' Real Health newsletter, you'll learn shocking truths about "junk medicine" and how to stay healthy while eating eggs, meat and other foods you love.

With the tips you'll receive from Real Health, you'll see your doctor less, spend a lot less money and be happier and healthier while you're at it. The road to Real Health is actually easier, cheaper and more pleasant than you dared to dream.

Subscribe to Real Health today by calling 1-800-981-7162 or visit the Real Health web site at www.realhealthnews.com. Use promotional code : DRHBDZZZ

If you knew of a procedure that could save thousands, maybe millions, of people dying from AIDS, cancer, and other dreaded killers....

Would you cover it up?

It's unthinkable that what could be the best solution ever to stopping the world's killer diseases is being ignored, scorned, and rejected. But that is exactly what's happening right now.

The procedure is called "photoluminescence". It's a thoroughly tested, proven therapy that uses the healing power of the light to perform almost miraculous cures.

This remarkable treatment works its incredible cures by stimulating the body's own immune responses. That's why it cures so many ailments--and why it's been especially effective against AIDS! Yet, 50 years ago, it virtually disappeared from the halls of medicine.

Why has this incredible cure been ignored by the medical authorities of this country? You'll find the shocking answer here in the pages of this new edition of Into the Light. Now available with the blood irradiation Instrument Diagram and a complete set of instructions for building your own "Treatment Device". Also includes details on how to use this unique medical instrument.

Rhino Publishing S.A.
www.rhinopublish.com

Into the Light

Into the Light

Dr. Douglass' Complete Guide to Better Vision

A report about eyesight and what can be done to improve it naturally. But I've also included information about how the eye works, brief descriptions of various common eye conditions, traditional remedies to eye problems, and a few simple suggestions that may help you maintain your eyesight for years to come.
-William Campbell Douglass II, MD

The Hypertension Report.
Say Good Bye to High Blood Pressure.

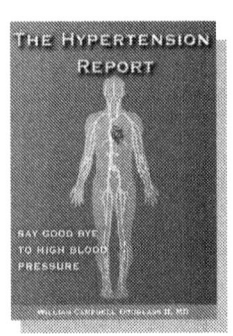

An estimated 50 million Americans have high blood pressure. Often called the "silent killer" because it may not cause symptoms until the patient has suffered serious damage to the arterial system. Diet, exercise, potassium supplements chelation therapy and practically anything but drugs is the way to go and alternatives are discussed in this report.

Grandma Bell's A To Z Guide To Healing With Herbs.

This book is all about - coming home. What I once believed to be old wives' tales - stories long destroyed by the new world of science - actually proved to be the best treatment for many of the common ailments you and I suffer through. So I put a few of them together in this book with the sincere hope that Grandma Bell's wisdom will help you recover your common sense, and take responsibility for your own health. -William Campbell Douglass II, MD

Prostate Problems:
Safe, Simple, Effective Relief for Men over 50.

Don't be frightened into surgery or drugs you may not need. First, get the facts about prostate problems... know all your options, so you can make the best decisions. This fully documented report explains the dangers of conventional treatments, and gives you alternatives that could save you more than just money!

Color me Healthy
The Healing Powers of Colors

"He's crazy!"
"He's got to be a quack!"
"Who gave this guy his medical license?"
"He's a nut case!"

In case you're wondering, those are the reactions you'll probably get if you show your doctor this report. I know the idea of healing many common ailments simply by exposing them to colored light sounds far-fetched, but when you see the evidence, you'll agree that color is truly an amazing medical breakthrough.

When I first heard the stories,
I reacted much the same way.
But the evidence so
convinced me, that I had to
try color therapy in my practice.
My results were truly amazing.

-William Campbell Douglass II, MD

Order your complete set of Roscolene filters (choice of 3 sizes) to be used with the "Color Me Healthy" therapy. The eleven Roscolene filters are # 809, 810, 818, 826, 828, 832, 859, 861, 866, 871, and 877. The filters come with protective separator sheets between each filter. The color names and the Roscolene filter(s) used to produce that particular color, are printed on a card included with the filters and a set of instructions on how to fit them to a lamp.

Rhino Publishing
www.rhinopublish.com

What Is Going on Here?

Peroxides are supposed to be bad for you. Free radicals and all that. But now we hear that hydrogen peroxide is good for us. Hydrogen peroxide will put extra oxygen in your blood. There's no doubt about that. Hydrogen peroxide costs pennies. So if you can get oxygen into the blood cheaply and safely, maybe cancer (which doesn't like oxygen), emphysema, AIDS, and many other terrible diseases can be treated effectively. Intravenous hydrogen peroxide rapidly relieves allergic reactions, influenza symptoms, and acute viral infections.

No one expects to live forever. But we would all like to have a George Burns finish. The prospect of finishing life in a nursing home after abandoning your tricycle in the mobile home park is not appealing. Then comes the loss of control of vital functions the ultimate humiliation. Is life supposed to be from tricycle to tricycle and diaper to diaper? You come into this world crying, but do you have to leave crying? I don't believe you do. And you won't either after you see the evidence. Sounds too good to be true, doesn't it? Read on and decide for yourself.

-William Campbell Douglass II, MD

Rhino Publishing S.A.
www.rhinopublish.com

HYDROGEN PEROXIDE
Medical Miracle
H₂O

Don't drink your milk!

If you knew what we know about milk... BLEECHT! All that pasteurization, homogenization and processing is not only cooking all the nutrients right out of your favorite drink. It's also adding toxic levels of vitamin D.

This fascinating book tells the whole story about milk. How it once was nature's perfect food...how "raw," unprocessed milk can heal and boost your immune system ... why you can't buy it legally in this country anymore, and what we could do to change that.

Dr. "Douglass traveled all over the world, tasting all kinds of milk from all kinds of cows, poring over dusty research books in ancient libraries far from home, to write this light-hearted but scientifically sound book.

The Milk Book

William Campbell Douglass II, MD

Rhino Publishing, S.A.
www.rhinopublish.com

Eat Your Cholesterol!

Eat Meat, Drink Milk, Spread The Butter- And Live Longer!
How to Live off the Fat of the Land and Feel Great.

Americans are being saturated with anti-cholesterol propaganda. If you watch very much television, you're probably one of the millions of Americans who now has a terminal case of cholesterol phobia. The propaganda is relentless and is often designed to produce fear and loathing of this worst of all food contaminants. You never hear the food propagandists bragging about their product being fluoride-free or aluminum-free, two of our truly serious food-additive problems. But cholesterol, an essential nutrient, not proven to be harmful in any quantity, is constantly pilloried as a menace to your health. If you don't use corn oil, Fleischmann's margarine, and Egg Beaters, you're going straight to atherosclerosis hell with stroke, heart attack, and premature aging -- and so are your kids. Never feel guilty about what you eat again! Dr. Douglass shows you why red meat, eggs, and dairy products aren't the dietary demons we're told they are. But beware: This scientifically sound report goes against all the "common wisdom" about the foods you should eat. Read with an open mind.

Rhino Publishing, S.A.
www.rhinopublish.com

The Joy of Mature Sex
and How to Be a Better Lover

Humans are very confused about what makes good sex. But I believe humans have more to offer each other than this total licentiousness common among animals. We're talking about mature sex. The kind of sex that made this country great.

Stop Aging or Slow the Process
How Exercise With Oxygen Therapy
(EWOT) Can Help

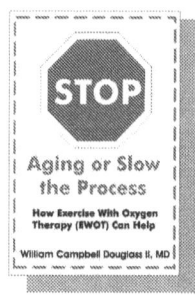

EWOT (pronounced ee-watt) stands for Exercise With Oxygen Therapy. This method of prolonging your life is so simple and you can do it at home at a minimal cost. When your cells don't get enough oxygen, they degenerate and die and so you degenerate and die. It's as simple as that.

Hormone Replacement Therapies:
Astonishing Results For Men And Women

It is accurate to say that when the endocrine glands start to fail, you start to die. We are facing a sea change in longevity and health in the elderly. Now, with the proper supplemental hormones, we can slow the aging process and, in many cases, reverse some of the signs and symptoms of aging.

Add 10 Years to Your Life
With some "best of" Dr. Douglass' writings.

To add ten years to your life, you need to have the right attitude about health and an understanding of the health industry and what it's feeding you. Following the established line on many health issues could make you very sick or worse! Achieve dynamic health with this collection of some of the "best of" Dr. Douglass' newsletters.

How did AIDS become one of the Greatest Biological Disasters in the History of Mankind?

GET THE FACTS

AIDS and BIOLOGICAL WARFARE covers the history of plagues from the past to today's global confrontation with AIDS, the Prince of Plagues. Completely documented *AIDS and BIOLOGICAL WARFARE* helps you make your own decisions about how to survive in a world ravaged by this horrible plague.

You will learn that AIDS is not a naturally occuring disease process as you have been led to believe, but a man-made biological nightmare that has been unleashed and is now threatening the very existence of human life on the planet.

There is a smokescreen of misinformation clouding the AIDS issue. Now, for the first time, learn the truth about the nature of the crisis our planet faces: its origin -- how AIDS is really transmited and alternatives for treatment. Find out what they are not telling you about AIDS and Biological Warfare, and how to protect yourself and your loved ones. AIDS is a serious problem worldwide, but it is no longer the major threat. You need to know the whole story. To protect yourself, you must know the truth about biological warfare.

PAINFUL DILEMMA

Are we fighting the wrong war?

We are spending millions on the war against drugs while we
should be fighting the war against pain with those drugs!

As you will read in this book, the war on drugs was lost a long time ago and,
when it comes to the war against pain, pain is winning! An article in USA Today
(11/20/02) reveals that dying patients are not getting relief from pain. It seems
the doctors are torn between fear of the government, certainly justified, and a
clinging to old and out dated ideas about pain, which is NOT justified.

A group called Last Acts, a coalition of health-care groups, has released a very
discouraging study of all 50 states that nearly half of the 1.6 million Americans
living in nursing homes suffer from untreated pain. They said that life was being
extended but it amounted to little more than "extended pain and suffering."

This book offers insight into the history of pain treatment and the current failed
philosophies of contemporary medicine. Plus it describes some of today's most
advanced treatments for alleviating certain kinds of pain. This book is not another
"self-help" book touting home remedies; rather, Painful Dilemma: Patients in
Pain -- People in Prison, takes a hard look at where we've gone wrong and what
we (you) can do to help a loved one who is living with chronic pain.

The second half of this book is a must read if you value your freedom. We now
have the ridiculous and tragic situation of people
in pain living in a government-created hell by
restriction of narcotics and people in prison for
trying to bring pain relief by the selling of
narcotics to the suffering. The end result of the
"war on drugs" has been to create the greatest
and most destructive cartel in history, so great,
in fact, that the drug Mafia now controls most
of the world economy.

Rhino Publishing S.A.
www.rhinopublish.com

Live the Adventure!

Why would anyone in their right mind put everything they own in storage and move to Russia, of all places?! But when maverick physician Bill Douglass left a profitable medical practice in a peaceful mountaintop town to pursue "pure medical truth".... none of us who know him well was really surprised.

After All, anyone who's braved the outermost reaches of darkest Africa, the mean streets of Johannesburg and New York, and even a trip to Washington to testify before the Senate, wouldn't bat and eye at ducking behind the Iron Curtain for a little medical reconnaissance!

Enjoy this imaginative, funny, dedicated man's tales of wonder and woe as he treks through a year in St. Petersburg, working on a cure for the world's killer diseases. We promise --

YOU WON'T BE BORED!

Rhino Publishing S.A.
www.rhinopublish.com

THE SMOKER'S PARADOX
THE HEALTH BENEFITS OF TOBACCO!

The benefits of smoking tobacco have been common knowledge for centuries. From sharpening mental acuity to maintaining optimal weight, the relatively small risks of smoking have always been outweighed by the substantial improvement to mental and physical health. Hysterical attacks on tobacco notwithstanding, smokers always weigh the good against the bad and puff away or quit according to their personal preferences. Now the same anti-tobacco enterprise that has spent billions demonizing the pleasure of smoking is providing additional reasons to smoke. Alzheimer's, Parkinson's, Tourette's Syndrome, even schizophrenia and cocaine addiction are disorders that are alleviated by tobacco. Add in the still inconclusive indication that tobacco helps to prevent colon and prostate cancer and the endorsement for smoking tobacco by the medical establishment is good news for smokers and non-smokers alike. Of course the revelation that tobacco is good for you is ruined by the pharmaceutical industry's plan to substitute the natural and relatively inexpensive tobacco plant with their overpriced and ineffective nicotine substitutions. Still, when all is said and done, the positive revelations regarding tobacco are very good reasons indeed to keep lighting those cigars - but only 4 a day!

Rhino Publishing, S.A
www.rhinopublish.com

Bad Medicine
How Individuals Get Killed By Bad Medicine.

Do you really need that new prescription or that overnight stay in the hospital? In this report, Dr. Douglass reveals the common medical practices and misconceptions endangering your health. Best of all, he tells you the pointed (but very revealing!) questions your doctor prays you never ask. Interesting medical facts about popular remedies are revealed.

Dangerous Legal Drugs
The Poisons in Your Medicine Chest.

If you knew what we know about the most popular prescription and over-the-counter drugs, you'd be sick. That's why Dr. Douglass wrote this shocking report about the poisons in your medicine chest. He gives you the low-down on different categories of drugs. Everything from painkillers and cold remedies to tranquilizers and powerful cancer drugs.

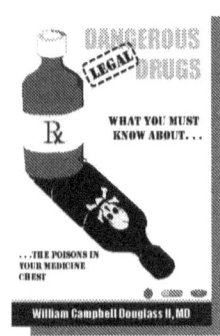

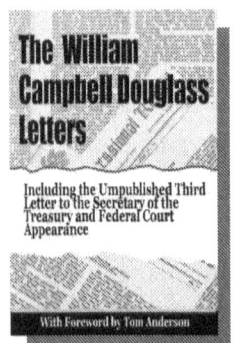

The William Campbell Douglass Letters.
Expose of Government Machinations
(Vietnam War).

THE WILLIAM CAMPBELL DOUGLASS LETTERS. Dr. Douglass' Defense in 1968 Tax Case and Expose of Government Machinations during the Vietnam War.

The Eagle's Feather. A Novel of
International Political Intrigue.

Although The Eagle's Feather is a work of fiction set in the 1970's, it is built, as with most fiction, on a framework of plausibility and background information. This is a fiction book that could not have been written were it not for various ominous aspects, which pose a clear and present danger to the security of the United States.

You want to protect those you love from the health dangers the authorities aren't telling you about, and learn the incredible cures that they've scorned and ignored?
Subscribe to the free Daily Dose updates "...the straight scoop about health, medicine, and politics." by sending an e-mail to real_sub@agoramail.net with the word "subscribe" in the subject line.

Rhino Publishing

ORDER FORM

PURCHASER INFORMATION

Purchaser's Name (Please Print): _____

Shipping Address (Do not use a P.O. Box): _____

City: _____ State/Prov.: _____ Country: _____

Zip/Postal Code: _____ Telephone No.: _____ Fax No.: _____

E-Mail Address (if interested in receiving free e-Books when available): _____

CREDIT CARD INFO (CIRCLE ONE):

MASTERCARD, VISA, AMERICAN EXPRESS, DISCOVER, JCB, DINER'S CLUB, CARTE BLANCHE.

Charge my Card -> Number #: _____ Exp.: _____

*Security Code: _____ * Required for all MasterCard, Visa and American Express purchases. For your security, we require that you enter your card's verification number. The verification number is also called a CCV number. This code is the 3 digits farthest right in the signature field on the back of your VISA/MC, or the 4 digits to the right on the front of your American Express card. Your credit card statement will show **a different name than Rhino Publishing** as the vendor.

WE DO NOT share your private information, we use 3$^{\underline{rd}}$ party credit card processing service to process your order only.

ADDITIONAL INFORMATION

If your shipping address is not the same as your credit card billing address, please indicate your card billing address here.

_____   Type of card: _____
Name on the card

Billing Address: _____

City: _____ State/Prov.: _____ Zip/Postal Code: _____

Fax a copy of this order to:
RHINO PUBLISHING, S.A.
1-888-317-6767 or International #: + 416-352-5126

To order by mail, send your payment by first class mail only to the following address. Please include a copy of this order form. Make your check or bank drafts (NO postal money order) payable to RHINO PUBLISHING, S.A. and mail to:

Rhino Publishing, S.A.
Attention: PTY 5048
P.O. Box 025724
Miami, FL.
USA 33102

Digital E-books also available online: www.rhinopublish.com

Rhino Publishing

ORDER FORM

Purchaser's Name (Please Print): _____

I would like to order the following paperback book of Dr. Douglass (Alternative Medicine Books):

___	X	9962-636-04-3	Add 10 Years to Your Life. With some "best of" Dr. Douglass writings.	$13.99 $ ___
___	X	9962-636-07-8	AIDS and Biological Warfare. What They Are Not Telling You!	$17.99 $ ___
___	X	9962-636-09-4	Bad Medicine. How Individuals Get Killed By Bad Medicine.	$11.99 $ ___
___	X	9962-636-10-8	Color Me Healthy. The Healing Power of Colors.	$11.99 $ ___
___	X	9962-636 -XX-X	Color Filters for Color Me Healthy. 11 Basic Roscolene Filters for Lamps.	$21.89 $ ___
___	X	9962-636-15-9	Dangerous Legal Drugs. The Poisons in Your Medicine Chest.	$13.99 $ ___
___	X	9962-636-18-3	Dr. Douglass' Complete Guide to Better Vision. Improve eyesight naturally.	$11.99 $ ___
___	X	9962-636-19-1	Eat Your Cholesterol! How to Live off the Fat of the Land and Feel Great.	$11.99 $ ___
___	X	9962-636-12-4	Grandma Bell's A To Z Guide To Healing. Her Kitchen Cabinet Cures.	$14.99 $ ___
___	X	9962-636-22-1	Hormone Replacement Therapies. Astonishing Results For Men & Women	$11.99 $ ___
___	X	9962-636-25-6	Hydrogen Peroxide: One of the Most Underused Medical Miracle.	$15.99 $ ___
___	X	9962-636-27-2	Into the Light. New Edition with Blood Irradiation Instrument Instructions.	$19.99 $ ___
___	X	9962-636-54-X	Milk Book. The Classic on the Nutrition of Milk and How to Benefit from it.	$17.99 $ ___

___ X ___	9962-636-00-0	Painful Dilemma - Patients in Pain - People in Prison.	$17.99 $ ___
___ X ___	9962-636-32-9	Prostate Problems. Safe, Simple, Effective Relief for Men over 50.	$11.99 $ ___
___ X ___	9962-636-34-5	St. Petersburg Nights. Enlightening Story of Life and Science in Russia.	$17.99 $ ___
___ X ___	9962-636-37-X	Stop Aging or Slow the Process. Exercise With Oxygen Therapy Can Help.	$11.99 $ ___
___ X ___	9962-636-60-4	The Hypertension Report. Say Good Bye to High Blood Pressure.	$11.99 $ ___
___ X ___	9962-636-48-5	The Joy of Mature Sex and How to Be a Better Lover...	$13.99 $ ___
___ X ___	9962-636-43-4	The Smoker's Paradox: Health Benefits of Tobacco.	$14.99 $ ___

Political Books:

___ X ___	9962-636-40-X	The Eagle's Feather. A 70's Novel of International Political Intrigue.	$15.99 $ ___
___ X ___	9962-636-46-9	The W. C. D. Letters. Expose of Government Machinations (Vietnam War).	$11.99 $ ___

SUB-TOTAL: $ ___

ADD $5.00 HANDLING FOR YOUR ORDER: $ 5.00 $ 5.00

___ X ___ ADD $2.50 SHIPPING FOR EACH ITEM ON ORDER: $ 2.50 $ ___

NOTE THAT THE MINIMUM SHIPPING AND HANDLING IS $7.50 FOR 1 BOOK ($5.00 + $2.50)
For order shipped outside the US, add $5.00 per item

___ X ___ ADD $5.00 S. & H. OR EACH ITEM ON ORDER (INTERNATIONAL ORDERS ONLY) $ 5.00 $ ___
Allow up to 21 days for delivery (we will call you about back orders if any)

TOTAL: $ ___

Fax a copy of this order to: 1-888-317-6767 or Int'l + 416-352-5126
or mail to: Rhino Publishing, S.A. Attention: PTY 5048 P.O. Box 025724, Miami, FL, 33102 USA
Digital E-books also available online: www.rhinopublish.com